Be an UNSTOPPABLE MOM

CINDY KAPPLER

© MMXXIII Cindy Kappler/Enzo Recommends and SBC Publishing

All Rights Reserved

Published in the United States of America by Enzo Recommends and SBC Publishing.

Cover Design: Izabel N @Izabeladesign

Limits of Liability/Disclaimer of Warranty

All rights reserved. No part of this book may be reproduced by any mechanical, photographic, or electronic process, or in the form of a phonographic recording; nor may it be stored in a retrieval system, transmitted, or otherwise be copied for public or private use - other than for "fair use" as brief quotations embodied in articles and reviews - without prior written permission of the publisher.

All links are for information purposes only and are not warranted for content, accuracy or any other implied or explicit purpose.

This book contains material protected under International and Federal Copyright Laws and Treaties. Any unauthorized reprint or use of this material is prohibited.

ISBN: 9798865282846

JOIN OUR FACEBOOK GROUP

HELLO UNSTOPPABLE MOM!

I'd love to have you join our "Be an Unstoppable Mom" Facebook group. You can participate in our discussions and keep up with all of the fun tips and strategies I share for being an Unstoppable Mom. Really, it's the feedback from the other moms that I enjoy the most and you may too.

Join us today!

Look for the "Be an Unstoppable Mom" group on Facebook.

VISIT THE BE AN UNSTOPPABLE MOM WEBSITE

I set up an easy to use Be an Unstoppable Mom Resource page for you. You'll find it at: http://www.BeAnUnstoppableMom.com/resources.

On the web page, you'll find links to all of the resources mentioned in this book, including links to downloadable PDF files for the Growth Work. Also, when I find new information I think will be helpful to you as an unstoppable mom, I post it in the Bonus section of the Resource page.

Stop by and take a look!

Also by Cindy Kappler

We're Pregnant! The Must-Have Pregnancy Book for Couples (co-authored by husband Eugene Kappler)

Written by the Kappler Kids
15 Reasons I Love My Dad, A Fill-in-the-Blank Book

Dedication

Family is everything. And without my family, I would not have been qualified to write a book about being an Unstoppable Mom.

Thank you, husband and life partner Eugene, and children Samantha, Benjamin, Kassi, Joshua and Nathaniel. I love you to the moon and back. You fill my heart with joy and make me smile each and every day.

Who is Cindy Kappler?

As a mother of five fun-loving, adventurous and confident children, I know firsthand the challenges and pressures that come with raising a family. From the chaos of everyday life to the juggling act of being a full-time working mom, I learned a lot along the way. And now, I want to share my wisdom and insights with you.

My qualifications as an unstoppable mom go beyond my personal experience with my own children. In addition to raising two daughters and three sons, I have been a certified teacher and school administrator so I understand the dynamics of parenthood from an educational perspective. I was also fortunate to be trained in Stephen Covey's Habits of Highly Successful Families, giving me a unique set of skills to help you navigate the complexities of motherhood. And true confessions, I was a huge fan of Super Nanny when the show was popular years ago.

Is the unstoppable mom in you shining through? Imagine a life where you feel less stress, you have more patience, and your outlook on life and motherhood is one of positivity and optimism. In "Be an Unstoppable Mom" you'll gain the knowledge and strategies to become "that mom", create a harmonious family environment, and cultivate a stronger connection with your children.

Let me inspire you to trust yourself and embrace the journey of motherhood. Discover your own unique strengths as a mom and embrace strategies you can use to raise confident, caring and resilient children.

Contents

Chapter 1
Be an Unstoppable Mom... 1

Chapter 2
Understanding Your Mindset
The Key to Unlocking the Power Within You............................. 9

Chapter 3
The Power of an Unstoppable Mom Mindset
Embrace the Journey, Learn from Each Experience
and Grow with Your Children... 19

Chapter 4
Mindset Mastery
Unleashing Extraordinary Results Through Simple Tweaks......... 33

Chapter 5
Rewiring Your Thoughts
Six Simple Steps to Reset Any of Your Mindsets So You Can
Have Less Stress, More Patience and Feel More Positive............ 49

Chapter 6
Mindset #1 - Cultivating a Growth Mindset
The Key to Being an Unstoppable Mom....................................... 59

Chapter 7
Mindset #2 - Harnessing Positivity
The Secret Ingredient of an Unstoppable Mom............................ 79

Chapter 8
Mindset #3 - Patience and Understanding
The Pillars of an Unstoppable Mom... 99

Chapter 9
Mindset #4 - Unconditional Love
The Compass of an Unstoppable Mom.. 117

Chapter 10
Mindset #5 - Mindful Presence
The Heartbeat of Connection in an Unstoppable Mom................ 137

Chapter 11
Mindset #6 - Role Modeling
The Living Lessons Taught by an Unstoppable Mom................... 161

Chapter 12
Mindset #7 - Self-Care
The Importance of Taking Care of Yourself
So You Can Be An Unstoppable Mom.. 181

Chapter 13
Harnessing the Power of the 7 Mindsets
Unleash the Unstoppable Mom in You... 199

Chapter 14
Next Steps: From Inspiration to Action
Navigating Life Beyond this Book as an Unstoppable Mom........ 207

Be an Unstoppable Mom

Chapter 1

Be an Unstoppable Mom

"The strength of a mother is the foundation on which a family thrives."
- J.K. Rowling

Welcome to the remarkable journey of "Be an Unstoppable Mom: Your Guide to Less Stress, More Patience, and a Positive Mindset While Raising Confident, Caring, and Resilient Children." In the bustling whirlwind of motherhood, we all share a common desire - to become that unstoppable mom who exudes poise, patience, and positivity, all while nurturing children who are confident, caring, and resilient. It's a vision that speaks to the heart of every mother.

As moms, we're no strangers to the ever-shifting roles and responsibilities that define our lives. We're nurturers, organizers, and dream-weavers. But amidst the chaos and constant demands, one question looms large: How can we be the moms we aspire to be while also tending to our own well-being?

This journey begins with a profound understanding: Your mindsets are your most potent tool. They hold the key to unlocking your full potential as a mom and as an individual. In the pages that follow, you will explore the incredible influence of your mindsets, discovering how they can pave the way to less stress, more patience, and an unwavering positivity that will enrich not only your life but also leave an enduring impact on your children.

Having a better understanding of who YOU are as you learn to master your mindsets is critical. Understanding why you think the way you do and why you respond the way you do will give you invaluable insights into your own thought processes and reactions. To gain this understanding, you will take a personality assessment and identify your grit score. These assessments will guide you on a journey of self-discovery, helping you understand your true self, your unique strengths, your preferences, and those areas where you may want to grow. Armed with this self-awareness, you'll be better equipped to tailor your parenting approach to your own personality, creating more intimate connections with your children.

As you delve into the essence of mindset, you'll gain an understanding of what a mindset is and why a growth mindset is more beneficial to you than a fixed one. This knowledge will serve as the cornerstone of your transformative journey. You'll discover why your mindsets are so powerful and how you can harness them to become the unstoppable mom you want to be – a mom who feels less stress, has more patience and sees the world with a positive outlook. You'll define what it truly means to be an unstoppable mom - someone who not only manages the demands of motherhood but thrives in the role, leaving an indelible legacy of confidence, compassion, and resilience in the hearts of your children. You'll look at the significant impact a few simple tweaks to your mindsets can have and learn the six-step process for modifying any of your many mindsets.

Then, once you have a solid understanding of what your mindsets are all about and the steps you can use to tweak them as needed, you will explore the seven mindsets that are crucial to being an unstoppable mom.

These mindsets are:

<u>Growth Mindset:</u> Understand the difference between a growth mindset and a fixed mindset, and see the profound impact these two mindsets

have on your ability to be the mom you want to be.

<u>Positive Mindset</u>: Uncover the significance of maintaining a positive outlook and how it equips you to overcome challenges with grace.

<u>Patience and Understanding Mindset</u>: Discover why patience and understanding are your allies in navigating the daily trials of motherhood, and fostering harmony and empathy in your family.

<u>Unconditional Love Mindset</u>: Explore the profound importance of unconditional love and how it nurtures your child's self-worth and emotional resilience.

<u>Mindful Presence Mindset</u>: Learn the art of being fully present in the moment, and how this mindset can reduce stress and deepen your connection with your children.

<u>Role Model Mindset</u>: Understand why you, as a role model, have the power to shape your child's character and values by demonstrating the behaviors you wish to see in them.

<u>Self-Care Mindset</u>: Delve into self-care as a non-negotiable aspect of your journey, exploring how it enables you to recharge, manage stress, and model self-love for your children.

As you learn about each mindset, you will determine which of the seven mindsets you want to work on. Tweaking just one mindset – like positivity, for example – can have an enormous impact on how you look at the world and how you interact with your children. Keep in mind, you don't have to change all of your mindsets, only the ones you know will be most impactful for you, your children and your family.

In each of the seven mindset chapters, you will find a discussion about the mindset and how it can make you an unstoppable mom. To help you get a true sense of the significant impact a mindset modification can have, each chapter includes a story about a mom who modified the mindset being discussed and the impact this change had on her. Each chapter also includes 15 to 20 examples you can model to strengthen your use of the specific mindset being discussed and three detailed actions you can take to practice each example.

For instance, in the positive mindset chapter, one example of what you can do to gain a more positive outlook and three specific actions you can take are:

Positive Self-Talk: You can harness positivity by being mindful of your internal dialogue. By challenging negative thoughts and replacing them with positive ones, you can maintain a more optimistic mindset.
- Internal Conversations: Make a conscious effort to be kind to yourself when engaging in discussions in your head. Become your own best friend and remind yourself of the things you like about yourself. This is a skill your children can learn and benefit from too.
- Challenge Negative Thoughts: When you catch yourself thinking negatively about yourself, consciously challenge those thoughts. Ask yourself if there is evidence to support these negative beliefs or if they are based on assumptions or insecurities. Replace negative thoughts with more balanced and constructive ones. For example, if you think, "I'm terrible at this," challenge it with, "I may be facing a challenge, but I can learn and improve."
- Practice Self-Compassion: Treat yourself with the same kindness and understanding that you would offer to a friend. When you make a mistake or face a setback, avoid harsh self-criticism. Instead, acknowledge your imperfections and shortcomings with compassion. Remind yourself that everyone makes mistakes, and these experiences are opportunities for growth and learning.

In each mindset chapter, I included examples and specific actions you can take to strengthen the mindset because I think that is one of the easiest ways to feel confident that you are taking the right steps. The examples and actions have been tested and proven. They work! You don't have to try all of them – just the ones you think will bring the most benefit to you and your children. If you're not sure, pick one that sounds good and give it a try. See how your children respond. See how it makes you feel. Try it a few more times and if you like what you're seeing, keep doing it. If not, try another action and see if that one gives you a response you like better.

At the end of chapters two through five, you will find Growth Work that contains links to recommended videos, the personality and grit assessments, and other activities that will be helpful to you on your unstoppable mom journey.

Whether you're an experienced mom seeking fresh perspectives or a new mom embarking on this incredible adventure, "Be an Unstoppable Mom" is your guide, your companion, and your source of inspiration. Together, we'll embark on a life-altering journey that empowers you as a mom. It's a journey that will also empower your children to become the confident, caring, and resilient individuals you know they can be. Learning to maximize your control over your own mindsets is a skill that will help you as a mom when your children are young and at home, and even when your children are grown and out of the house.

Are you ready to unleash the unstoppable mom within you? Let's dive in and get started.

Chapter Summary

• **Embark on Your Journey**: You are on a path to becoming an unstoppable mom, learning to balance the whirlwind of motherhood with poise, patience, and positivity while raising confident, caring, and resilient children.

• **Harness Your Mindsets:** Discover the power of your mindsets. They are your tools for less stress and more patience, impacting not just your life but also your children's growth and happiness.

• **Understand Yourself:** Engage in a journey of self-discovery through a personality assessment and grit score. Understanding yourself better enables you to tailor your parenting approach to your unique strengths and areas for growth.

• **Embrace a Growth Mindset:** Learn about the growth mindset and its advantages over a fixed mindset. This knowledge is the cornerstone of your transformation as a mom.

• **Master Seven Key Mindsets:** Explore and master one or more of the seven mindsets that are essential to your journey as an unstoppable mom: Growth, Positivity, Patience and Understanding, Unconditional Love, Mindful Presence, Role Modeling, and Self-Care.

• **Apply Practical Examples and Take Action:** In each mindset chapter, you'll find examples and specific actions you can incorporate into your daily activities to bring the mindset to life for you and your children. Try them! The results may surprise you.

- **Access Resources for Continuous Growth:** Benefit from resources and growth work provided in the book and on our resource page at www.BeAnUnstoppableMom.com/Resources. You'll find videos, assessments, and additional helpful information to aid you on your unstoppable mom journey.

- **The Purpose of "Be an Unstoppable Mom":** This book is a guide and source of inspiration tailored to you, helping you empower not just yourself but also your children to become the confident, caring, and resilient individuals you know they can be.

Chapter 2

Understanding Your Mindset
The Key to Unlocking the Power Within You

"Your most valuable parenting skill is learning to manage yourself first."
- Dr. Laura Markham

Motherhood is a journey filled with unparalleled joys, but it's also riddled with challenges that can be overwhelming. From sleepless nights to juggling multiple responsibilities, it's easy to feel stressed and lose sight of the sheer beauty of being a mother. Fortunately, there is a powerful tool that you can control and easily call upon to guide you – your mindsets. Understanding your many mindsets is the key to unlocking the hidden power within you and using that power to reduce your stress, increase your patience and help you to develop a more positive outlook in all you do.

A mindset, in its simplest form, is the lens through which you perceive and interpret the world. It's not just a fleeting thought; it's the foundation upon which your attitudes, actions, and decisions are built. You have an overall mindset that drives most of what you say and do - this is usually referred to as a fixed or growth mindset. Within this main mindset you have many other mindsets that are specific to your thoughts, ideas and experiences.

UNDERSTANDING YOUR MINDSET

Your mindsets play a pivotal role in virtually everything you do in life, from how you approach challenges and view success to how you interact with others and shape your own self-concept. Your mindsets are the set of beliefs and attitudes that influence your behavior and your outlook on life.

Everything you do and say is a reflection of your mindsets. For this reason, the importance of your mindsets cannot be overstated. Your mindsets can either empower you to move forward and excel – or hold you back and slow you down.

Despite the importance of your mindsets, you may not actively think about the lenses through which you view the world. If this is true, you are not alone. In spite of its profound influence, many people do not consciously think about their mindsets. They are not aware of how the voice inside their head may be influencing what they say and how they act, both positively and negatively.

For a long time, I was not consciously aware of my mindsets. I just responded to things as they came. And that worked pretty well for me. But then I stumbled across this quote:

> *"I may not be able to control what happens to me,*
> *but I can control how I respond to it."*

That really got me thinking about my own actions and how much I did or did not control them. Let me clarify - of course I control my own responses and actions, no one else can. But did that mean I was really aware of how I was going to respond or what I was going to do? And if not, what inside my head was driving my responses and actions?

This quote suggests the idea that while you can't always dictate the events or circumstances that unfold in your life, you have control over your reactions and responses to them. The quote encourages a mindset shift from focusing on what is beyond your control to focusing on what you can control – your attitudes and responses. Such a shift demonstrates a growth mindset. It shows that you know you can adapt your response to an event even though you may not be able to control the event itself. Conversely, letting the situation control you and dictate your response without you thinking you can have an impact demonstrates a fixed mindset.

This takes us back to the idea that people have either a fixed or a growth mindset. How does a fixed or growth mindset impact you as a mom?

Moms juggle a lot every day, including a multitude of mindsets that pop up when least expected - such as your mindset about being positive, your mindset about being patient and even your thoughts on unconditional love. Your overall mindset, whether fixed or growth-oriented, can significantly impact your ability to modify your many other mindsets. Here's why...

A fixed mindset is a belief system or attitude where an individual perceives their abilities, intelligence, and personal qualities are static and unchangeable traits. People with a fixed mindset tend to believe their potential is predetermined, and they have a limited capacity for improvement. As a result, they may avoid challenges, fear failure, and tend to give up easily when faced with difficulties, as they believe their efforts won't make a significant difference. This mindset can hinder personal growth and resilience, and the willingness to embrace opportunities for learning and development.

If a mom has a fixed mindset, she is likely to accept what comes her way with the thought that she cannot change her lot in life. For example, a mom with a fixed mindset may say she is always tired. Instead of trying to understand why she might be tired and then trying to make a change - maybe she stays up late, or wakes up often during the night or only gets a few hours of sleep each night - she simply accepts that she will always be tired and there is nothing she can do about it. Through her actions, words and expectations, she will likely share this fixed mindset with her children. This may result in her children growing up with a fixed mindset too, a mindset that says, "Things happen to me and there isn't anything I can do about it."

On the opposite spectrum, individuals with a growth mindset - a concept developed by psychologist Carol Dweck[1] - see challenges as opportunities for growth, view failure as a natural part of the learning process, and are more likely to embrace difficulties with resilience and determination. They believe in the power of practice and continuous learning to expand their potential, leading to a greater willingness to take on new challenges and a stronger sense of self-confidence. A growth mindset fosters a love for learning and enables individuals to reach higher levels of achievement and personal development.

A mom with a growth mindset is more likely to be open to trying to identify the cause of a problem and then trying to figure out how to fix it. In the previous example, a mom with a growth mindset might look at her sleep habits and try to see if there is something she can change that will let her sleep more and therefore be less tired. She might try going to bed earlier or sleeping more hours each night.

A growth mindset can make a mom more adaptable and receptive to feedback, which is essential in recognizing and addressing any fixed beliefs or behaviors she wants to change. Through her actions, words and expectations, she will likely share this growth mindset with her children. This will result in her children growing up with a growth mindset like their mom, and realizing they have the ability to change things for the better if they want to and are willing to put in the effort.

A fixed or growth mindset can also have a huge impact on how a mom responds to her children. A mom with a fixed mindset might believe that her children's abilities and intelligence are fixed from birth, leading her

---

1. Dweck, C.S. (2008) Mindset. Ballantine Books.

to have lower expectations or doubt her children's potential to strengthen and improve their skills and abilities. A mom with a fixed mindset who has a child who struggles to read might accept that her child is not going to be a good reader. Instead of encouraging her child to practice reading by finding a topic she enjoys reading about, or sitting down and reading with her, the mom may tell the child reading just isn't her strength.

On the other hand, a mom with a growth mindset believes that her children can develop their skills and strengthen their abilities through practice and effort. She will encourage her children to embrace challenges, persevere through failures, and see setbacks as valuable learning experiences. If her child struggles to read, a growth minded mom will seek out ways to help her child improve her reading skills. She will encourage her child to practice reading and help her find something she enjoys reading so reading becomes more interesting to the child.

Ultimately, the difference lies in how a mom's mindset shapes her approach to parenting by either limiting or fostering her children's potential for growth and resilience. A mom with a growth mindset is better equipped to modify her own mindset because she's more inclined to see personal growth as something she can do. She's willing to learn, adapt, and make the necessary changes to model a growth-oriented mindset for her children, ultimately fostering a healthier and more resilient family environment. Ideally, a mom should embrace and work towards a growth mindset.

In addition to the fixed vs. growth mindset, there are six additional mindsets that are extremely important to you as a mom:
- A Positive Mindset
- A Patient and Understanding Mindset
- An Unconditional Love Mindset
- A Mindful Presence Mindset

- A Role Model Mindset
- A Self-Care Mindset

We will discuss each of these mindsets, including the growth mindset, in detail as you move through the book. You will also see examples of what each of the mindsets looks like in the day-to-day life of an unstoppable mom like you.

When you take control of one or more of your mindsets, you make a conscious decision to act and react in a certain way. If you choose to have a positive mindset, your actions and reactions will come from a place of positivity, optimism and hope. If you choose to have a patient and understanding mindset, your actions and reactions will come from a place of empathy, compassion and consideration for others. The mindsets you choose to adopt and focus on are the ones that will guide your actions and reactions.

The good news is it is definitely possible for you to change your mindset in any area. And changing your mindset can absolutely change your results.

Adopting and developing a growth mindset is important in your journey to become the absolute best mom you can be. Recognizing and actively cultivating a healthy and growth-oriented mindset can be transformative. It may require introspection, self-awareness, and a willingness to challenge long-held beliefs and assumptions. While this may sound like a lot of work, the rewards of being in tune with your mindsets are immense and can lead to personal and professional growth, increased resilience, and improved overall life satisfaction. You can model these attributes for your child, showing them not only how to grow and learn but also how to navigate the world with curiosity, perseverance and joy.

Your mindsets are more than just a set of beliefs. They are a powerful tool that not only shapes your journey through motherhood but through your entire life. By embracing a growth mindset, you become an unstoppable force, capable of nurturing, teaching, and loving in the most empowering ways.

Chapter Summary

- **Motherhood is a Journey**: The motherhood journey comes with both joys and challenges. Being able to understand and manage your mindsets is a powerful tool for reducing stress and fostering a patient and positive outlook.

- **Mindsets are Your Lens to the World**: Your many mindsets serve as the lenses through which you perceive and interpret the world. Your mindsets influence your attitudes, actions, and decisions.

- **Growth Oriented or Fixed Mindset**: Your overall mindset, whether fixed or growth-oriented, significantly impacts all aspects of your life, from how you approach challenges to how you view your self-concept.

- **Fixed Mindset vs Growth Mindset**: If you have a fixed mindset, you will see your abilities as static. This can hinder your personal growth, resilience, and willingness to embrace challenges. If you have a growth mindset, you will view challenges as opportunities for growth and embrace difficulties that come your way with resilience.

- **The Importance of a Mom's Mindset**: Your mindset as a mom, whether fixed or growth-oriented, affects your ability to modify your other mindsets and influence the development of your children's mindsets.

- **The Most Important Mindsets for a Mom**: In addition to the fixed vs. growth mindset, there are six additional important mindsets for moms to embrace. These mindsets are positivity, patience and understanding, unconditional love, mindful presence, role modeling, and self-care.

- **Owning Your Mindsets**: Taking control of your own mindsets involves conscious decisions on your part to act and react in specific ways, leading to transformative results in your personal and professional growth.

- **Embrace a Growth Mindset**: Embracing a growth mindset in motherhood fosters adaptability, resilience, and joy, making you an unstoppable force capable of nurturing, teaching, leading and loving in many different ways.

***

Growth Moment: Do I Have a Growth Mindset?

Visit the Resource page at http://www.BeAnUnstoppableMom.com/resources where you will find links to two videos that describe in great detail the difference between a growth mindset and a fixed mindset. The videos focus on identifying whether you have a fixed or growth mindset and on 11 strategies you can adopt as you work to develop or strengthen your own growth mindset.

Chapter 3

The Power of an Unstoppable Mom Mindset

Embrace the Journey, Learn from Each Experience and Grow with Your Children

> *"There's no way to be a perfect mother and a million ways to be a good one."*
> – Jill Churchill

Being unstoppable means embodying a mindset of resilience, determination, and unwavering commitment to achieving your goals. It's about approaching challenges with a positive, can-do attitude and viewing obstacles not as roadblocks but as opportunities for growth and learning.

An unstoppable individual does not equate success with a lack of failure. Instead, they understand that failure is an integral part of the journey to success. They don't shy away from mistakes but embrace them as valuable lessons that provide insight and pave the way to improvement.

Being unstoppable also means possessing a steadfast belief in yourself and your abilities. This self-confidence fuels motivation, drives perseverance, and empowers you to push beyond your perceived limits. In essence, to be unstoppable is to possess the grit, resilience, and tenacity to keep going despite setbacks or difficulties, constantly striving for growth and progress.

An unstoppable mom is a mother who embodies resilience, determination, and strength in her approach to parenting. She is not defined by perfection but by her relentless pursuit of growth, both for herself and her children. She faces every challenge with courage and every success with humility, constantly adapting and learning from every situation. Such moms are unstoppable not because they never stumble, but because every time they fall, they pick themself up and continue forward, stronger than before.

An unstoppable mom mindset goes beyond merely navigating the challenges of motherhood. It is about embracing the journey, learning from each experience, and growing alongside your children. It is a mental framework that a mother adopts to approach parenting with strength, determination, and constant growth.

An unstoppable mom mindset includes a profound dedication to motherhood, characterized by an assortment of qualities that foster a nurturing, patient, positive, and enabling environment for your child's growth. An unstoppable mom mindset empowers mothers to approach every challenge with courage and determination, always prioritizing their child's needs. This mindset also helps a mom to feel less stress, have more patience and to see the world in a more optimistic light.

An unstoppable mom mindset is one of balance, wisdom and unending love. It is one of compassion and growth. It's about facing the complexities of motherhood with grit and grace, constantly learning, adapting, and striving to provide the best for your child while also taking care of your own well-being. It's about being unstoppable not because there are no obstacles, but because you are able to rise above them, time and again. It's about creating an environment where children feel loved, understood, and encouraged to be the best versions of themselves.

Not all unstoppable moms share the same mindsets but they do have many in common. Mindsets often seen in unstoppable moms include a growth mindset, a positive outlook, patience and understanding, an ability to give unconditional love, mindful presence, an awareness that as a mom you serve as a role model at all times to your children, and the knowledge that self-care makes an unstoppable mom even more unstoppable.

What do these mindsets look like when embodied by an unstoppable mom?

A Growth Mindset is shown by an unstoppable mom when she promotes a culture of learning, resilience, and continuous improvement within her family, modeling behaviors that nurture self confidence and the pursuit of personal growth. It's a belief that abilities and understanding can be developed through dedication and hard work. A mom with a growth mindset teaches her children that effort is a path to mastery and that it's okay to make mistakes, as these are crucial steps in learning. Embracing a growth mindset allows a mom to model resilience, perseverance, and a love of learning for her children. It encourages her to approach each stage of her child's development - and her own personal growth as a parent - with openness, curiosity, and a commitment to continuous learning and adaptation. A child whose mother has a growth mindset sees that he or she has the ability to improve and strengthen almost anything he or she wants to. The child sees that his own effort makes a huge difference in the outcome. He gains confidence in his own abilities and becomes more resilient when faced with a challenge. I strived to model and encourage a growth mindset to my children. It warms a mom's heart to see their children adopt what they teach. My daughter Kassi played basketball in junior high. She didn't play in many games, but she practiced hard and was determined to play in high school. Having a growth mindset, Kassi knew practice and dedication would improve her skills. Kassi's future high school held summer practices every weekday evening from 5 to

7 pm. Kassi attended almost every practice all summer long. When tryouts started, she had improved significantly and confidently joined the group of girls trying out for the team. As an in-coming freshman, Kassi made the team - and played high school varsity basketball all four years. Her growth mindset gave her the belief that she could improve her skills and the confidence to try.

A Positive Mindset is shown by an unstoppable mom as her positivity serves as a guiding light through life's challenges. Her unwavering belief in the power of optimism allows her to tackle even the toughest of obstacles with a smile. Her positivity sets an inspiring example for her family. Her boundless determination and unyielding hope shape her children's outlook, teaching them to embrace life's ups and downs with grace and gratitude. An unstoppable mom radiates positivity, illuminating the path forward for herself and those she loves, proving that a positive mindset is not just a choice but a way of life. Children who live with a mom who sees things in a positive light become more positive themselves. They see the glass as half full and view their world with an "I can do" attitude. I am a very positive person and definitely wanted to teach my children to focus on the positive side of things whenever possible. At our house, we always tried to do things "with a happy heart". Homework, dinner dishes, laundry, raking - whatever the task, I encouraged my children to go at it with a happy heart. Rather than being annoyed or frustrated about having to do something and dragging themselves through it, they looked at each task as something they had to do but didn't need to be unhappy about doing. Hence, they did things with a happy heart. If one child would fuss about a task, it was very likely another would remind them to do it "with a happy heart." When you take on a task with a happy heart, you feel better about doing it and time seems to pass much faster.

A Patient and Understanding Mindset is shown by an unstoppable mom when she embodies patience and understanding as the cornerstones of her parenting journey. In the whirlwind of raising children and navigating the complexities of family life, she remains steadfast in her ability to listen without judgment, empathize with her children's struggles, and offer unwavering support. Her calm demeanor and gentle guidance create a safe space for her family to express their thoughts and feelings, nurturing open communication and trust. Through her own experiences and the challenges she faces as a mother, she demonstrates that patience is important and understanding is the bridge that connects hearts and minds. An unstoppable mom's ability to foster patience and understanding within her family is a testament to her enduring love and tireless dedication to their well-being. A child who learns to be patient and understanding sees the world and everyone around her in a kind and caring way. She is compassionate, she is encouraging and she sees the best in others. She is like a magnet, drawing others to her because she knows how to listen, share and play nicely. Patient and understanding children grow up to be patient and understanding parents. While it is not always the fastest way to resolve an issue or the easiest way to talk to your child, pausing for a moment to ask questions so you truly understand what has happened can give you so much more clarity about a situation and help you to come to the right conclusion. Seeking to understand is a valuable skill, especially when you have more than one child. I always told my children they had to answer my many questions because there are two sides to every story and the truth is usually somewhere in the middle. I never expected anyone to intentionally mislead me but just like adults, each child sees a situation differently and it can take time to sort out what really did happen.

An Unconditional Love Mindset is shown by an unstoppable mom when she loves her children fiercely and without conditions, and she provides them with a sense of safety, comfort, and unwavering support. A mother's love is limitless, no matter the circumstances. Unconditional love lays the foundation for a strong emotional bond between a mother and her child. This sense of secure attachment helps a child grow confident, resilient, and emotionally intelligent. It's a fundamental tenet of an unstoppable mom mindset, serving as a source of constant motivation. When showing unconditional love, a mom showers her child with love that doesn't waver or fade, regardless of the circumstances or her child's behavior. This boundless affection creates a secure and comforting foundation for the child's development. Someone once told me they will always love their child but that doesn't mean they will always like what their child does. I took that to heart and when appropriate, used the phrase with my children, reminding them that "I will always love you but right now I do not like the behavior you are doing."

A Mindful Presence Mindset is shown by an unstoppable mom when she is present in every moment with her child, understanding that it's the quality of time, not just the quantity, that matters most. She recognizes the value of shared experiences. She believes in the power of 'now'. She is fully present and attentive during interactions with her child, creating meaningful connections and memories. This mindful presence strengthens the mother-child bond and encourages children to value the moment. A child whose mom practices mindful presence knows she values him. He knows that when he is with his mom, she is truly there - listening to him, paying attention to him and appreciating him. He knows that when he and his mom make plans, share ideas or work through a challenge - his mom is focused on him and the topic they are discussing. His mother's mindful presence teaches him to be present when interacting with others and reinforces his mother's unconditional love for him. Children are very aware of times when their mom is not showing them mindful presence. My children made a game out of talking to me when I was working on the computer. They would ask for something and I would respond, without stopping what I was doing or giving them my attention. It didn't take too many times of me saying "Who said you could do that?" and them replying "You, when you were on the computer" to learn the importance of stopping, looking and listening when talking to my children.

A Role Modeling Mindset is seen when an unstoppable mom recognizes that she is her child's first and most influential role model and consciously displays behaviors and attitudes she wants her child to emulate. This includes demonstrating positivity, patience, kindness, resilience in the face of adversity, empathy, respect for others, and self-care, among other traits. Whether we like it or not, our children model what they see and hear - good or bad. I will never forget being at a Walmart with my adorable three-year old daughter. She saw something that surprised her and in her loudest, most grown-up baby voice yelled "What the #*&@!" She certainly got the attention of those who were near us. I can truthfully say I don't speak that way but my daughter's daddy occasionally does. Children do model what they see and hear!

A Self-Care Mindset is seen in an unstoppable mom when she acknowledges and understands that taking care of herself is not just essential, but a priority. It's about acknowledging that self-care is not an act of indulgence or selfishness, but a necessary practice to maintain mental, emotional, and physical well-being. As moms, we often set aside our needs to take care of those we love. You encourage your husband or partner to relax, rest or go out with the guys. You make sure your children have down time and get to play, watch television, read a book or take a fun class. But often, you don't do the same for yourself. You should! Think about the last time you made a conscious effort to do something that you find fun, relaxing or entertaining. How did it make you feel? Hopefully, you felt refreshed...energized...and ready to take on anything that might come your way. My friend Furzana says she is all about self-care and being SELF-ish. Self-care has nothing to do with being selfish and everything to do with caring for your self. As a mom, you give and give and give all day long. To be the unstoppable mom you want to be, you have to make sure to not only take great care of your family but to also take good care of yourself. As a role model for your children, you want to make sure they grow up seeing that everyone - including mom - needs some time for self-care. And you want them to see that your self-care revitalizes you so you can give even more to them.

Each of these seven mindsets serves a unique purpose in nurturing children and guiding them as they grow into positive, confident, caring, independent, well-rounded individuals.

In the following chapters, we will discuss how small tweaks to any of your mindsets can give you extraordinary results. We will explore each of the seven mindsets in more depth, providing real-life examples of what they look like in the day-to-day life of an unstoppable mom.

Cultivating Grit:
Nurturing Resilience and Perseverance

Before we move on, I've mentioned the word grit a few times. What is grit?

According to Angela Duckworth[2]: "Grit is passion and perseverance for long term goals. Grit is having a goal you care about so much that it organizes and gives meaning to almost everything you do." To assess how gritty a person is, Duckworth created an assessment called the Grit Scale that gives a person a score between one and five, based on their responses to a series of questions.

A score of one means a person has very little grit and likely will not stay focused on a particular project or goal for very long. They may be easily distracted or simply get tired of what they are working on and move on to something else. If completing the project is difficult or the goal takes a great deal of effort to accomplish, they are likely to stop and put their focus somewhere else.

A score of five means a person is very gritty. They are likely to take on a project or set a goal and keep working at it until they complete it or

---

2. Duckworth, A. (2016) Gift: The power of passion and perseverance.

meet it. The degree of difficulty or the amount of time required is not likely to stop them. They are steadfast and focused on doing what it takes to complete their objective.

What does the Grit Scale mean for a mom?

While the Grit Scale assessment isn't designed specifically for moms, it can provide valuable insights to anyone, including moms, about their perseverance and passion for their life goals, which can extend to their parenting journey. Here's what the Grit Scale can tell a mom:

When it comes to her level of perseverance, the grit assessment can help a mom understand how determined and persistent she is in pursuing her goals, whether they are related to her career, personal interests, or parenting. The assessment can reveal whether she is likely to stick with her commitment and overcome challenges that come up.

A mom will find that grit is closely tied to resilience, and the assessment can shed light on how well she bounces back from setbacks. A mom with a high grit score may be more resilient in the face of challenges, which can be particularly beneficial in the demanding role of motherhood.

When it comes to role modeling, which moms do every day, if the assessment reveals that a mom has a high level of grit, it reinforces the importance of being a positive role model for her children. When a mom demonstrates grit in her own life, she can inspire her kids to develop determination and resilience. High grit can inspire children to adopt a similar mindset of perseverance and passion, setting them on a path to stick with things they start, and to set and achieve their own goals.

A gritty mom exhibits several characteristics and behaviors that reflect her determination and commitment to her role as a mother. It's important to note that no mom is gritty all the time, and gritty moms come in all personality types and backgrounds. Grit is a quality that can be cultivated and expressed in different ways. What sets gritty moms apart is their determination to grow, adapt, and persist in their roles as mothers while pursuing their personal goals and passions.

A mom's grittiness can vary from one area of her life to another or from one goal to another. A mom can have a high level of grit in one area and much less in others. For example, when it comes to potty training, a mom can be very gritty in her desire to potty train her child. With her focus on getting rid of diapers and having her child gain some independence in the bathroom, a mom may set up a potty schedule and stick to it at all times, putting intense focus on teaching her child to use the potty. In another area, perhaps the morning routine for waking up and getting ready for school, the same mom may take a much more laid back, less structured approach, as she is not as focused or concerned about the morning routine as she was about potty training.

Angela Duckworth's grit assessment can give a mom insights that can be applied to her parenting journey, guiding her in fostering resilience, setting an example for her children, and balancing her own goals with her responsibilities as a mother.

For an unstoppable mom, the concept of grit is a powerful ally, enabling you to navigate the complexities of parenting with determination and perseverance.

Chapter Summary

• **Embrace Resilience and Determination**: As an unstoppable mom, embody resilience, determination, and a commitment to your goals. Approach challenges with a positive attitude, seeing them as growth opportunities.

• **Learn from Failure:** Understand that failure is a part of your journey to success. Embrace mistakes as lessons, using them to gain insight and allow for growth.

• **Believe in Yourself:** Possess a strong belief in your abilities. This self-confidence motivates you, drives perseverance, and pushes you beyond perceived limits.

• **Know the Value of Grit and Tenacity in Motherhood:** As an unstoppable mom, show resilience, determination, and strength in parenting. Embrace growth for both yourself and your children. Approach each challenge with courage and confidence.

• **Cultivate a Range of Positive Mindsets:** Adopt mindsets like a growth mindset, positivity, patience, unconditional love, and mindfulness. These mindsets create a nurturing environment for both your child's growth and your own.

• **You Need Balance and Wisdom as a Mom:** Face motherhood's complexities with grit and grace, learning and adapting constantly to provide the best for your child while also caring for yourself.

• **Use Grit to Overcome Parenting Challenges:** Understand grit as passion and perseverance for long-term goals. Use Angela Duckworth's grit assessment to gauge your determination and resilience, applying these insights to your parenting journey.

***

Growth Moment: How Gritty Am I? And What Do My Personality Traits Tell Me?

As you embark on your journey to develop your unstoppable mom mindset, it may be helpful to know what your grit score is and thus know how gritty you are. When you see your grit score, click on the More About Grit link to learn more about grit and how and when your grit level can impact your life.

Keep in mind that your grit score can change over time and can change depending on the task, project, or goal you are working on. Each of us have certain things that we are so passionate about, we would do anything to keep them or accomplish them. A grit level for such a project could easily be a five whereas for many other areas of our life, our grit score could be closer to the middle or lower end of the grit spectrum.

Your grit score is not set in stone. You can develop more grit if you choose to do so.

What's your grit score? Visit the Resource page at http://www.BeAnUnstoppableMom.com/resources where you will find a link to the Grit Scale assessment.

***

Additionally, many moms find it fascinating to complete a personality test to find out how their specific thoughts and beliefs may impact their motherhood journey. I personally think this can be thought-provoking and eye-opening.

If you are interested, I recommend a free version of the well-known Myers-Briggs Type Indicator (MBTI) personality assessment[3].

The MBTI assessment is made up of a series of statements and takes about 20 minutes to complete. For each statement, indicate how well it applies to you on a scale from Strongly Agree to Strongly Disagree. Do not overthink your answers as it is best to go with your initial gut response.

The objective of taking the MBTI is for YOU to understand your natural tendencies. It is not about how you think others will expect you to behave in specific situations. Be you!

The assessment categorizes people into 16 personality types. Each personality type gives insights into how a person sees the world, makes decisions and interacts with their surroundings. Once you complete the MBTI, you will be given detailed information about your results. The information will be broken down into categories like parenting, relationships, work, etc.

Like any personality assessment, it isn't perfect but chances are you will be surprised at how close it comes to identifying what makes you who you are. The most informative part comes from reading the results and hearing how a mom with your personality type typically acts in the role of parent, partner, employee, friend, etc.

You will find a link to the free MBTI personality assessment on our Resource page at http://www.BeAnUnstoppableMom.com/resources.

---

3. Briggs, Katharine C. (1987). Myers-Briggs type indicator. Form G.

Chapter 4

Mindset Mastery
Unleashing Extraordinary Results Through Simple Tweaks

"Parenting is the easiest thing in the world to have an opinion about but the hardest thing in the world to do."

- Anne Lamoti

What if you change your mindset about your mindsets?

Think about your mindsets as the steering wheel of your life. When you are driving, just a small adjustment to the direction you are going can lead to a massive change in where you end up. In the same way, a few tweaks to any one of your mindsets can bring about significant transformations in your life.

For example, if you tend to look at life from a glass-half-empty viewpoint you can decide that you want to change to a more positive outlook and see the glass as half-full. This will impact your positivity mindset. Similarly, if you become impatient easily and want to work on having more patience, you will be working to strengthen your patience and understanding mindset.

Keep in mind that tweaking a mindset is not always easy; it requires self-awareness, patience, and perseverance. However, even small changes can have a cascading effect, eventually leading to substantial personal growth and improved life satisfaction. In the example above, if you decide you want to be more patient, perhaps you could start by not getting frustrated in the morning when your kids are struggling to get ready for school. How do you do this? Focus on being patient, not raising your voice, being encouraging and slowing down a little. Help yourself do this by consciously changing the morning routine to remove things that cause you to be impatient.

Children do well with routines, once they learn them. A routine lets them know what to expect and when. An effective routine implemented consistently can be a game changer!

If you don't already, have the kids pick out their clothes the night before, have them help pack their lunch and have them get their backpack ready for school - all before they go to bed. This will save time in the morning. And you will avoid feelings of being impatient while your children search for their clothes, decide what they want for lunch, and struggle to find and get everything in to their backpacks. It's already done! Your children will feel less rushed and so will you.

You can make an even bigger impact on your morning by changing the morning routine so you get up 15 minutes earlier and get yourself ready for work before your children wake up. This will ensure you are ready to go without feeling like you have to hurry. Maybe you have to get up 30 minutes before your children but you get the idea! Give yourself time to make sure you are ready to go before getting your children up.

Make the morning even less stressful by turning on music so the kids wake up to their favorite songs. You could dance your way into their room to get them out of bed. This should put a smile on everyone's face. And as soon as they are out of bed, the kids can get the clothes they laid out the night before and get dressed.

When I started using these strategies with my children, it made such a difference! First, since I made sure I was ready to walk out the door before I woke my children up, I was not stressed or worried about me being ready to go. Big relief! And preparing the night before by choosing clothes, packing lunches and getting backpacks ready to go saved us so much time and grief in the morning. We had hooks for everyone's backpack - backpacks were always on their hook unless it was homework time or time to pack the backpack. We never had to look for backpacks. And getting clothes ready meant making sure all clothes - including shoes, socks and jackets - were picked out and ready to wear. My clothes were picked out too!

As soon as I was ready to go, I would turn on our favorite songs and the house would be filled with uplifting toe-tapping music. My children could hear the music in their bedrooms and after a few weeks of moaning and groaning about getting up, they started to get out of bed and get dressed when the music played. It was a joy to see and our mornings became calm and peaceful.

Don't forget breakfast. We had fresh fruit, cereal, granola bars, frozen waffles and yogurt easily accessible. The older children got their own and either they or I helped the younger ones. Once a child was ready to go to school they were free to do what they chose until departure time. When it was time to leave, I would give a five minute warning and at that point, they would finish what they were doing, get their backpacks and head to the van.

When my children were young - four kiddos age eight or younger at one time - it took more planning, effort and time on my part to make our routine work. But as they got older, each child took on more responsibility for making sure they were ready to go and often helped their siblings. The time put into creating and learning a morning routine was nothing compared to the time we saved, and the frustration and impatience we avoided every day.

You might not be able to make all these changes at one time, but imagine how your morning routine could change for the better if you slowly implemented some of these time-saving patience-preserving actions!

Give yourself permission to adjust your mindsets, embrace the learning process and witness the transformation that follows. The process of changing one of your mindsets isn't an overnight shift; it takes time, patience, and a commitment to personal growth. But even minor tweaks in how you perceive yourself, your children, your partner, and the world around you can have a significant impact and turn you into an unstoppable mom. Embracing this change can lead to healthier relationships, a happier family, and a more relaxed and confident you.

Take a deep breath, get ready to adjust your mental steering wheel, and watch as the changes ripple out, improving every aspect of your life. The following are a few examples of the impact mindset modifications can have:

Altering your mindset can change your perspective. Shifting from a fixed to a growth mindset allows you to see challenges not as obstacles, but as opportunities for growth and learning. This change in perspective can let you actively look for solutions, enabling you to overcome difficulties more efficiently and with less stress.

Imagine a mom who dreads getting her kids to bed every night - many parents do! She will approach bedtime with feelings of avoidance and anxiety. But what if she changes the way she looks at her children's bedtime routine and thinks about how to make it fun? Instead of watching the clock tick towards bedtime with apprehension and a desire to be anywhere but there, she can change the way she looks at bedtime and create a routine that is fun, focused and successful (thus taking on a growth mindset about bedtime). This simple shift in her mindset about bedtime will decrease her stress level, give her more patience and make her feel much more optimistic as bedtime approaches. The process of getting everyone to bed will become easier for all.

This mom might decide to follow the bedtime routine we looked at earlier that includes making and packing lunches, getting backpacks packed up and ready, and helping children pick out their clothes. But why would she stop there? She can create a bedtime routine that actually gets her children into bed and ready to go to sleep by expanding the routine to include bath time, teeth brushing and bathroom visits. Then everyone can settle down for ten to fifteen minutes of story time or individual reading before she has them snuggle into bed. Using a routine like this, bedtime becomes something this mom looks forward to instead of something she wants to avoid.

I used a similar night time routine with my children. Bedtime became organized, productive and enjoyable. As noted, chaotic mornings of "Where are my socks?" "I can't find my backpack?" and "What should I take for lunch?" became well-organized mornings that got five kids and me up and ready to walk out the door on time and with a smile almost every day. Creating and consistently following a night and a morning routine reduced unnecessary stress and made our lives so much simpler.

Tweaking your mindset can impact your behavior. A change in the way you think can lead to a change in the way you act. For instance, by adopting a more positive mindset, you might find yourself reacting to situations with a calmer demeanor and making decisions that contribute to a more positive environment. This behavioral change not only benefits you but also those around you. Consider a mother who often finds herself reacting negatively to the everyday challenges at home - maybe it's the constant mess, the kids not listening, or just the endless to-do list. This constant negativity might make her feel drained, stressed, and less confident in her role as a mother. Her children will feel her stress and may begin to model her negative approach as they react to the world around them.

However, if this mom consciously decides to shift her mindset to a more positive one, things can change significantly. Instead of focusing on the mess, she might start to see it as a sign of a home that's lively and full of active, curious children. Instead of getting frustrated when the kids don't listen, she could take it as an opportunity to teach them about the importance of respect and communication. This positive mindset shift can help her approach these situations with a sense of calm and purpose, rather than stress and frustration. By reacting positively instead of negatively, this mom can contribute to a more peaceful, loving home environment, which will also have a positive effect on her children's behavior and their way of responding to things in their life.

A shift in mindset can also enhance your self-confidence. By believing in your ability to grow and improve, you empower yourself. You become more willing to take risks, venture out of your comfort zone, and seize opportunities that you might have previously avoided. This increase in self-confidence can open doors to new experiences and possibilities. For example, some moms feel overwhelmed by the chaos of managing a home, kids, and possibly a job - leading to low self-confidence, high levels of stress, and frustration. A mom in this situation might believe she's "just not a good mom" because she can't do everything perfectly all the time. This is a fixed mindset.

If this mom shifts to a growth mindset, she can look at these areas of her life in a different way - through a mindset that gives her the belief that she can make things better and the confidence to try new strategies to change how she does things at home. She might start to understand that every mother faces challenges and that struggling at times doesn't make her a bad mom. Instead of aiming for perfection, she could focus on small, achievable goals, like spending quality time with her children each day, or managing to keep a routine. As she meets these goals and sees the positive impact on her family - kids who feel loved and cared for, a more organized home, and a better work-life balance - her self-confidence will naturally grow. She'll understand that being a good mom doesn't mean being perfect, it's about growing, learning, and giving her best effort to her family. This shift in mindset can help boost her self-confidence tremendously.

And finally, a tweak in your mindset can significantly impact your relationship with your children, your spouse or significant other, and family and friends. By cultivating a patient and understanding mindset, you foster healthier, more supportive relationships with those around you. Imagine a mother who initially reacts to her child's outbursts or mistakes with frustration and criticism, creating a tense atmosphere at home. She might believe that she's teaching her child important lessons about behavior and responsibility, but the impact may often be a child who feels misunderstood and unsupported, leading to even more issues.

If this mom consciously shifts to a more patient and understanding mindset, the impact can be profound. Instead of reacting immediately with frustration when her child misbehaves, she begins to take a moment to consider her child's feelings and perspectives. She acknowledges that his outbursts might be a way of expressing emotions he doesn't fully understand or can't articulate and she tries to understand the reasons behind them. Similarly, she tries to understand what is causing her child to make mistakes, rather than focusing on the mistake itself. With this new mindset, she approaches these situations differently. She talks to her child calmly, helping him understand and express his emotions. She uses mistakes as teaching moments, showing her child how to take responsibility and learn from these instances. As a result, her child feels understood and supported, leading to fewer outbursts, better communication, and a more positive relationship. The mother, witnessing these positive changes and her child's increased trust in her, experiences a boost in her confidence and satisfaction in her parenting. The shift to a patient and understanding mindset not only improves her child's behavior but also her relationship with her child and her self-confidence as a mother.

While we're talking about your mindsets, if you are a working mom (aren't we all?) - let's take a quick look at how minor tweaks to your mindsets can positively impact your professional life since your mindsets plays a significant role in shaping your actions, reactions and overall performance away from home too.

Just a few tweaks to your mindset can bring about profound changes in your work and interactions with your coworkers. Think about this...

Change in Perspective: Altering your mindset can shift your perspective on work challenges. For example, if you adopt a growth mindset, you can look at work challenges through the lens of "How can I do this better?" or "What training do I need to meet the expectations of my boss?" This new viewpoint can make you more resilient, adaptable, and open to new ideas, enhancing your problem-solving skills and positively influencing your work output. As a boss in several different organizations, I always appreciated the initiative of an employee who took the time to ask how they could do something better or understand it more.

Improved Relationships: Tweaking your mindset to become more patient and understanding can have a significant impact on your relationships with your coworkers. You're more likely to approach conflicts constructively, communicate effectively, and foster a more collaborative and supportive work environment.

Enhanced Performance: By adopting a positive and optimistic mindset, you can significantly improve your work performance. You become more focused, motivated and productive, leading to higher-quality outputs. Additionally, your optimism can rub off on your coworkers, enhancing team morale and overall productivity.

Increased Confidence: A mindset shift towards self-belief and confidence can make you more assertive, allowing you to voice your ideas and opinions more freely. This confidence can lead to increased recognition and opportunities at work, and can also inspire your coworkers to express themselves more openly.

Better Work-Life Balance: If you tweak your mindset to prioritize balance, you can manage your work and personal life more effectively. This balance can lead to reduced stress, higher job satisfaction and improved relationships, both at work and at home.

Take a moment to consider the following example of a mom who consciously worked to change her mindset to become an unstoppable mom:

Sophia, a mother of two spirited twins, found herself constantly overwhelmed and stressed. The constant juggle between work, her children's needs, and household chores left her feeling drained and irritable. Recognizing this wasn't the kind of mother she wanted to be, she decided to make a change.

The first step for Sophia was acknowledging her mindset. She realized she had fallen into a pattern of reacting to her situation instead of proactively managing it. Her mindset was primarily negative, focusing on the challenges she faced rather than the joy she could derive from her life. She decided to take up a regular mindfulness practice, incorporating meditation into her daily routine. This gave her a sense of calm and a space to reflect on her thoughts and attitudes. Sophia then began a deliberate practice of gratitude. Each night, she would write down three things she was grateful for, no matter how small. This shifted her focus from what was going wrong to what was going right. Next, Sophia made a conscious effort to reframe her challenges as opportunities. The mess her children made wasn't just a chore to clean up but a sign of their creativity and enjoyment. Her work wasn't just a source of stress, but also a source of personal fulfillment and a means to provide for her family.

Over time, Sophia saw dramatic changes. She was calmer, more patient with her children, and even more efficient at work. Stressful situations didn't seem as overwhelming as they once did. She became a model of resilience for her children, demonstrating that challenges can be met with patience and a positive attitude.

In adopting an unstoppable mom mindset, Sophia transformed not just her own experience of motherhood, but also the environment in her home, creating a more peaceful and joyful space for her family. It wasn't an overnight change, but her persistent efforts to change her mindset resulted in a powerful transformation.

Changing your mindsets into unstoppable mom mindsets isn't an overnight process, but even small adjustments can create a significant impact over time. By being mindful of your mindsets and taking steps to optimize them like Sophia did, not only will you positively impact your children, your spouse and yourself, you can also bring about transformative improvements in your work and relationships with your coworkers too.

Chapter Summary

• **Adjust Your Mindset:** Think of your mindsets as a steering wheel. Small adjustments can lead to significant changes in your life, just like a slight turn of your car's steering wheel can significantly change where you end up.

• **Small Tweaks to Your Mindset Can Have a Big Impact:** Changing your mindset, even in small ways, can have a cascading effect, leading to personal growth and improved life satisfaction. For instance, shifting from a pessimistic to a more optimistic outlook, or from a mindset of impatience to one of patience, can transform how you approach life.

• **Changing Your Mindset Requires Effort:** Keep in mind that altering a mindset takes self-awareness, patience, and perseverance. Changing your mindset is not always easy, but it is worth the effort for the transformative impact it can have.

• **Your Mindsets Influence You as a Mom:** As a mom, your mindsets profoundly influence how you perceive and react to parenting challenges, how you nurture your children and the kind of role model you become. Tweaking your mindsets can significantly transform your relationships and your approach to motherhood.

• **Changing Your Mindsets Results in Shifts in Your Perspective and Behavior:** Changing your mindsets can change your perspective. For example, try viewing challenges as opportunities. This can make you more resilient and adaptable and impact your behavior, leading to calmer reactions from you and a more positive environment for you and your family.

- **Your Mindsets Can Boost Your Self-Confidence and Strengthen Your Relationships:** A shift in your mindsets can enhance your self-confidence, making you more willing to take risks and seize opportunities. Mindset shifts can also improve your relationships with your children and spouse by fostering patience and understanding.

- **Mindset Tweaks Can Benefit Your Professional Life:** Minor adjustments in your mindsets can positively impact your professional life, enhancing your problem-solving skills, improving your relationships with coworkers, and increasing your job satisfaction and performance.

***

Growth Moment: Is this who you want to be?

Take a few minutes to complete the questions below. Write your answers in a notebook or on a piece of paper you can keep for comparison later. These notes are for you, to help you identify who you currently are and who you would like to be when it comes to your mindsets.

You will find a fillable PDF form containing the questions below on our Resource page at http://www.BeAnUnstoppableMom.com/resources.

You can refer to the following short definitions of each of the seven mindsets as you work your way through the questions.

Growth Mindset: A belief in the ability to develop skills and understanding through dedication and hard work, exemplified by a mom who fosters a culture of learning and resilience within her family, teaching her children the value of effort and the acceptance of mistakes as part of the learning process.

Positive Mindset: Demonstrated by an unwaveringly optimistic mom who navigates life's challenges with a smile, inspiring her family to embrace optimism, resilience, and a "can-do" attitude towards both successes and setbacks.

Patient & Understanding Mindset: Embodied by a mom who prioritizes patience and empathy in her parenting, creating a nurturing environment where open communication and trust flourish, ultimately fostering kindness, compassion, and resilience in her children.

Unconditional Love Mindset: Illustrated by a mom's boundless love and unwavering support for her children, regardless of circumstances or behavior, laying the foundation for their emotional well-being, confidence, and resilience throughout life.

Mindful Presence Mindset: Reflected in a mom's commitment to being fully present and attentive in every moment with her child, nurturing meaningful connections and reinforcing her child's sense of value, love, and security.

Role Modeling Mindset: Recognized by a mom's conscious effort to model positive behaviors and attitudes for her children, serving as a powerful influence in shaping their character, values, and actions through her own example.

Self-Care Mindset: Exemplified by a mom's acknowledgment of the importance of prioritizing her own well-being, inspiring her children to recognize the value of self-care and setting an example of balance and rejuvenation in their lives.

Your Mindset Assessment

1. Do you believe you have a fixed mindset or a growth mindset when it comes to challenges and personal development?

2. Which mindset (fixed or growth) do you aspire to have and why?

3. Do you think you would see any differences in your parenting if you adopted a growth mindset or if you developed your existing growth mindset even more? Explain your reasoning.

4. For each of the following mindsets, note whether you are happy with how the mindset reflects itself in your attitudes, actions and behaviors and why.
    a. Growth
    b. Positivity
    c. Patience and Understanding
    d. Unconditional Love
    e. Mindful Presence
    f. Role Modeling
    g. Self-Care

5. For each of the following mindsets, give an example of an attitude, action or behavior you exhibit as a result of your current mindset
    a. Growth
    b. Positivity
    c. Patience and Understanding
    d. Unconditional Love
    e. Mindful Presence
    f. Role Modeling
    g. Self-Care

6. Do you like the attitude, action or behavior you gave as an example in Item 5 or would you like to change it? Why do you/don't you like it and why would you/don't you want to change it?
    a. Growth
    b. Positivity
    c. Patience and Understanding
    d. Unconditional Love
    e. Mindful Presence
    f. Role Modeling
    g. Self-Care

7. For each of the following mindsets, are you content with your view of this mindset or do you want to change it? Why are you content or why aren't you content?
    a. Growth
    b. Positivity
    c. Patience and Understanding
    d. Unconditional Love
    e. Mindful Presence
    f. Role Modeling
    g. Self-Care

8. For each of the following mindsets, how do you believe your current mindset influences the way you encourage and support your children in their growth and development? Is this a good influence or one you would like to change and why?
    a. Growth
    b. Positivity
    c. Patience and Understanding
    d. Unconditional Love

e. Mindful Presence
   f. Role Modeling
   g. Self-Care

9. Having read this far in Be an Unstoppable Mom, is there anything you have noted that you want to incorporate into your role as an unstoppable mom? Is there any specific mindset you want to work on? If there is, what will you do to work on that specific mindset?

Chapter 5

Rewiring Your Thoughts
Six Simple Steps to Reset Any of Your Mindsets So You Can Have Less Stress, More Patience and Feel More Positive

> *"Being a mother is learning about the strengths you didn't know you had, and dealing with the fears you didn't know existed."*
> – Linda Wooten

Every person is different and every person has different mindsets that impact their reactions and emotions. Which of the seven mindsets has the biggest impact in your life? Start there. You may want to adjust your mindset relating to positivity or your patience and understanding mindset. Take it one step at a time and don't overwhelm yourself. Choose one mindset to work on that you feel will have the biggest impact on you as a mom and on your relationship with your children. Focus on that one mindset and use the steps below to rewire your brain and reset your mind.

As noted earlier, it won't happen overnight but in most cases, within three to four weeks, you should be feeling more comfortable with your new approach. Changing your mindset is like creating a new habit. Experts say it can take up to two months to turn a new behavior into an automatic response. The time will pass quickly. It always does!

You can rewire your mindset in five to six easy steps starting with awareness and then moving on to understanding, challenging yourself, reframing, practice, and seeking outside help (if needed). Follow these six simple steps to reset any mindset you want to change:

1. <u>Become Aware</u>: This is the first and perhaps most crucial step in changing your mindset. It's about self-reflection and identifying your current thought patterns and beliefs. For example, a mom named Ava often feels inadequate and overwhelmed. She constantly thinks, "I'm not a good enough mother because I can't keep the house spotless," and "I'm letting my children down because I'm too exhausted to play with them after a long day at work." Without realizing it, Ava has developed a negative mindset that impacts her feelings, behavior, and ultimately her perception of her self-worth. To start the process of changing her mindset, Ava needs to become aware of the negative feelings and recurring thought patterns she is having that are contributing to her feelings of being inadequate and overwhelmed.

2. <u>Understand</u>: The step of "understanding" entails gaining insight into the origins and sources of your beliefs, emotions, and thought patterns. It involves delving into the roots of why you have certain beliefs and why specific emotions arise in particular situations. This understanding helps you recognize the underlying causes of your thoughts and feelings, which is a crucial step in addressing and reshaping your mindset. Ava's thoughts may stem from many sources including societal expectations, personal perfectionism, or comparing herself to other moms she sees at work, her children's school and even on social media. Understanding where her thoughts come from can help Ava separate herself from these unhealthy standards. Once Ava recognizes these destructive thought patterns, she can begin to understand that these are not absolute truths, but rather reflections

of her mindset. Recognizing that mindsets can be changed is an empowering realization.

3. <u>Challenge Yourself</u>: Challenging your beliefs is the next crucial step in the process of changing your mindset, as it involves questioning and reevaluating the assumptions and convictions that may be holding you back. Ava, like many moms, may have internalized certain beliefs about motherhood that are causing her stress and self-doubt. For instance, she might have believed that the cleanliness of her house is a direct measure of her mothering skills. This belief can be particularly burdensome because it sets unrealistic expectations for her. As Ava begins to challenge this belief, she takes a closer look at its accuracy. She asks herself: Is it genuinely an accurate measure of my mothering skills if I can't keep the house clean all the time? As Ava begins questioning this limiting belief, she starts to recognize that the answer is no. Mothering is about so much more than the spotless state of her home. It's about nurturing, teaching, and creating a loving and supportive environment for her children. The cleanliness of the house is just one aspect of that environment, and it should not define her entire mothering experience. Ava may also believe that feeling tired after work is a sign that she's not a good mother. This belief can be particularly damaging because it can lead to burnout and neglect of her own well-being. However, by questioning this belief, she realizes that exhaustion is a natural part of being a working mother. It doesn't diminish her love or dedication to her children. Instead, it highlights the importance of self-care and acknowledging her own needs through this process of self-reflection and challenging her limiting beliefs, Ava begins to break down the power these beliefs have held over her. She starts to embrace a more compassionate and realistic perspective on motherhood, one that values her efforts and acknowledges that

perfection is neither achievable nor necessary. By letting go of these limiting beliefs, she opens herself up to a mindset that fosters positivity, self-acceptance, resilience, and a deeper sense of fulfillment in her role as a mother. This lets Ava focus on the things that are truly important to her and her children.

4. <u>Reframe Your Beliefs</u>: Reframing your beliefs is a powerful step in changing your mindset and fostering a more positive and empowering outlook. This step involves replacing limiting beliefs with more positive and empowering ones. Rather than holding on to the limiting belief that the cleanliness of her house is a measure of her worth or ability as a mother, Ava can consciously choose to replace this limiting belief with a more positive and empowering one such as "The cleanliness of my house doesn't define my worth or skill as a mother. Our home is a lived-in space, full of love and activity." In this new belief, Ava recognizes that her home is a place where her family creates memories, shares love, and experiences life together. It's a lived-in space, full of laughter, learning, and genuine moments. This perspective shift or reframing helps her see that the state of her home is not a reflection of her worth but rather a testament to the vibrant and active family life she's cultivating. Ava can also reframe her belief about feeling exhausted after work. Instead of seeing this as a sign of weakness or inadequacy, she can choose to believe: "Feeling exhausted after work is normal. I express love for my children in countless ways, and it's okay to need rest." With this reframe, Ava acknowledges that parenthood is a demanding role, and it's entirely normal to feel tired after a long day of work and caring for her children. She emphasizes that her love and care for her kids are demonstrated in a variety of ways beyond just her physical energy, and taking the time to rest and recharge is not only acceptable but necessary for her well-

being. Reframing beliefs like these can be transformative, allowing moms like Ava to embrace the imperfect but loving and joyful nature of motherhood while recognizing the importance of self-care and self-compassion.

5. <u>Practice</u>: Practice is key to any form of change, and altering your mindset is no exception. One key to changing your mindset is to change the discussion in your mind every time it goes to the thought you do not want. In Ava's case, once she has reframed her thoughts about how clean the house has to be and allowed herself to see that being tired when she comes home is okay, then every time those thoughts come negatively into her mind, she should immediately and consciously change the discussion in her head. She can change the discussion by repeating her reframed thought in her head, "The cleanliness of my house doesn't define my worth or skill as a mother. Our home is a lived-in space, full of love and activity" or reminding herself that "Feeling exhausted after work is normal. I express love for my children in countless ways, and it's okay to need rest." In this way, she opens her mind to the positive thoughts she wants and closes her mind to the negative thoughts that are bringing her down. Ava can and should repeat her new empowering beliefs to herself every day. She might write them down in a journal, say them out loud to herself each morning, or use them as mantras during meditation. It takes time for these new thoughts to become the default, but with consistent practice, they will.

6. <u>Seek Help, If Needed</u>: Change can be difficult to navigate alone. If needed, Ava might consider seeking support from a professional, like a psychologist, a counselor, or a life coach. These professionals can provide additional strategies, offer fresh perspectives, and encourage

progress. Alternatively, Ava might find support in a trusted friend, partner, or fellow parent. While moms are often hesitant to ask for help, it is always okay to seek feedback, guidance and support.

Use these six steps to reset your mindset in any area that you choose to address. Take it one step at a time and give yourself some grace as you work to make your new mindset a natural part of who you are. You will be amazed at the results.

***

The next seven chapters each focus on one specific mindset. As you read about each mindset, take note of the many examples and specific actions you can take to reinforce that mindset. Think about your own interactions with your children and if it's a mindset you want to work on, choose at least one action and try it.

As previously noted, simple tweaks can make a huge difference. Changing the way you do just one thing can have a significant impact on the interactions between you and your children.

Keep in mind - Every mom needs to choose the mindsets that will bring the most value to her life. You don't have to master all seven mindsets to become unstoppable. Pick and choose the ones that you believe will make the most difference to you, your children and your family, and then try them out. Don't try to change everything at once. Give yourself time to take on one mindset at a time.

Want to know more about each mindset? Read through the first few pages of each mindset chapter to get a better understanding of what each mindset is about.

Remember also that change takes time. You may not get the result you want the first, second or third time, but over time and with consistency, you will start to see positive changes. The process may not always be smooth and there may be some setbacks, but that doesn't mean failure. It's about making progress, not striving for perfection. Change takes time and patience. If you consistently apply the strategies in this book, you will be pleasantly surprised by the results.

Chapter Summary

- **Identify and Focus on One Key Mindset at a Time:** Begin by identifying one mindset you believe will most positively impact your role as a mom and your relationship with your children. Focus on changing this one mindset so you can see results and avoid feeling overwhelmed.

- **Use These Six Steps to Rewire Your Mindset:**
  1. Become Aware: Recognize and acknowledge your current mindset and thought patterns. Reflect on how these thoughts influence your emotions and behaviors.
  2. Understand: Dig into the origins of your beliefs. Understand why you think and feel a certain way, whether it's due to societal expectations, personal experiences, or other factors.
  3. Challenge Yourself: Question and reevaluate your beliefs. Consider if they are truly accurate and helpful or if they are limiting your potential.
  4. Reframe Your Beliefs: Replace negative or limiting beliefs with positive and empowering ones. This reframing helps in shifting your perspective towards a more constructive and optimistic outlook.
  5. Practice: Regularly reinforce your new, positive mindset. Consistently remind yourself of your reframed beliefs, using them as mantras or affirmations.
  6. Seek Help, If Needed: Don't hesitate to seek support from professionals or trusted individuals if you find it challenging to make these changes on your own.

- **Apply What You Learn to Each Mindset:** As you go through chapters 6-12 and focus on specific mindsets, apply the six steps to each mindset you want to modify. Use the examples and actions provided for each mindset to reinforce and model the mindset in your interactions with your children.

- **Take One Step at a Time:** Don't try to tackle all seven mindsets at once. Prioritize the ones that will bring the most value to you and your family, and work on them one at a time.

- **Be Patient and Persistent:** Remember that change takes time and effort. You might not see immediate results, and there may be setbacks, but consistency and perseverance will lead to positive changes.

- **Embrace Progress Over Perfection:** Understand that the goal is progress, not perfection. Every small step forward is a success in itself. With time and patience, mindset changes can transform your approach to motherhood and life.

***

Growth Moment: Use the Six Step Process to Reset One Mindset

Although we haven't yet reviewed in detail the seven mindsets that can make you an unstoppable mom, we have discussed them and you have read several examples of moms experiencing situations directly related to their mindset.

Go back to Question 9 in the Chapter 4 Growth Moment. You were asked to identify a mindset you want to work on. Knowing what you know now and thinking about that mindset, go through the six step process to reset your mindset and write down what you will do for each step.

Step 1: Become Aware (Use self-reflection to identify your current thought patterns and beliefs)

Step 2: Understand (Gain insight into the origins and sources of your beliefs, emotions, and thought patterns)

Step 3: Challenge Yourself (Question and reevaluate the assumptions and convictions that may be holding you back)

Step 4: Reframe Your Thoughts (Replace limiting beliefs with more positive and empowering ones)

Step 5: Practice (Repeat the action, affirmation or reframing thought over and over)

Step 6: Seek help, if needed (Seek support from a professional, like a psychologist or a life coach, or from a trusted friend, partner or other parent.)

You will find a fillable PDF form containing the six steps on our Resource page at http://www.BeAnUnstoppableMom.com/resources.

Chapter 6

Mindset #1 - Cultivating a Growth Mindset
The Key to Being an Unstoppable Mom

> *"Successful mothers are not the ones that never struggled. They are the ones that never give up, despite the struggles."*
> – Sharon Jaynes

Embarking on the journey of motherhood is extraordinary. It is filled with joy, challenges, triumph, and yes, learning opportunities. A crucial element to the success of your journey are the mindsets with which you approach your role as a mom. Cultivating a growth mindset — understanding that skills, abilities, and intelligence can be developed through your effort — can profoundly impact your mothering dynamics.

In motherhood, a growth mindset implies recognizing and cherishing your own evolution and that of your child. You aren't born with a predefined set of mothering skills, nor does your child arrive with an instruction manual. Don't you wish they did!

As an unstoppable mom with a growth mindset, you understand that you, your children, and your abilities are not static; they can grow and develop over time. You view challenges as opportunities for learning rather than insurmountable obstacles.

As an unstoppable mom, you acknowledge that this journey involves

MINDSET #1 - CULTIVATING A GROWTH MINDSET

continuous learning, adaptation, and growth. You allow yourself to be a novice, to make mistakes, to learn from them, and to improve. You appreciate the fact that as your children grow and change, so too must your parenting strategies. Unlike a fixed mindset that views capacities as predetermined, your growth mindset facilitates resilience and flexibility—vital qualities for unstoppable motherhood.

When you apply a growth mindset to your child's development, you cultivate an environment that promotes learning and exploration. You understand that your child is an individual on their own growth trajectory with the capacity to continually learn and develop.

As a mother with a growth mindset, you resist the temptation to label or pigeonhole your children. Instead, you emphasize effort, perseverance, and strategy. You inspire your children to view challenges as opportunities for growth rather than as threats. In the face of difficulty or failure, you guide your children to focus on what can be learned, fostering resilience and an enduring love of learning.

Your growth mindset becomes particularly crucial when you face challenges. Every mother encounters hurdles, whether they concern their child's behavior, academic performance, social interactions, or emotional well-being. As a mother with a growth mindset, you view these challenges not as evidence of failure but as opportunities for learning and growth. You adapt your strategies, seek advice, learn new skills, and help your children turn obstacles into stepping stones. This approach not only enhances your effectiveness as a mother but also models adaptive problem-solving behavior for your children.

Cultivating a growth mindset also extends to your personal growth. As a mother, you're more than your parenting role. You're an individual with your own interests, passions, goals, and potential for growth. As an unstoppable mom, you understand this. You know that your personal growth is not only beneficial to you but also to your children. When your children see you learning, growing, and overcoming your own challenges, they internalize the message that growth and learning are lifelong processes that extend beyond academic or professional realms.

The ripple effects of your growth mindset on your family can be profound.

Children nurtured in a growth mindset environment are more likely to develop a growth mindset themselves. They learn that their abilities can be developed, that effort leads to growth, and that challenges are opportunities for learning. This mindset fosters resilience, confidence, adaptability, caring, and a lifelong love of learning, equipping your children with vital skills for personal and professional success.

My growth mindset definitely rubbed off on my oldest daughter, Samantha. She is an amazing Cosplay costume designer. Over the years, I have watched her gain confidence and skills for designing and making the most realistic, beautiful or grotesque (depending on the character), eye-popping costumes. Samantha gives great attention to detail and meticulously adds one piece of the costume at a time. She has gone into costume contests with her costume taped, stapled, glued, pinned, tied, wired and paper-clipped together but that makes no difference to her. She performs on stage as if every piece was perfectly connected. Her costumes are extremely difficult to create but her growth mindset lets her begin each one knowing she can learn the skills she needs to make it perfect!

The adoption of a growth mindset is a cornerstone of unstoppable motherhood. This mindset allows you to evolve with your children, respond adaptively to challenges, foster your children's learning and resilience, and model lifelong learning. While the journey of motherhood is undeniably complex and demanding, approaching it with a growth mindset can transform being a mom into a gratifying journey of shared growth and discovery. Your growth mindset as a mom can take many forms, reflecting the belief that you and your children can develop skills, abilities, and intelligence through effort and perseverance.

As an example of the impact a mom with a growth mindset has on her children, let's take a look at a story about a mom named Susan:

Susan was a loving wife and a dedicated mother of two. She had always harbored a secret desire to learn tap dance, but life's responsibilities had always managed to keep her away from pursuing her passion. The thought of not having enough time or not being skilled enough had held her back for years.

One morning, as she sipped her coffee and gazed out the kitchen window, Susan had an epiphany. She realized that life was too short to keep postponing her dreams. She decided it was time to adopt a growth mindset and take the leap. She knew she could learn to tap, it would just take time and effort. Without any hesitation, she signed up for tap dance classes at a local dance studio.

Susan's decision to follow her dream came as a complete surprise to her children and her husband. They were accustomed to seeing her as the dedicated homemaker who always put their needs before her own. But they were thrilled to see her pursue something she was passionate about.

The first day of tap dance class was both exciting and nerve-wracking for Susan. She was surrounded by people who had been dancing for years, and she felt like the odd one out. But her newfound growth mindset kept her going. She practiced diligently and embraced every mistake as an opportunity to learn and improve.

Six weeks passed, and Susan's dedication began to pay off. Her tap dancing skills were improving, and she was becoming more confident with each passing day. Her children and husband noticed the positive change in her attitude. She had become an inspiration to them, showing them that it's never too late to chase your dreams and overcome self-doubt.

The big day arrived, and Susan had her first recital. Her family was in the audience, eagerly waiting to see her perform. As the spotlight shone on her, Susan's heart raced, but she didn't let fear hold her back. She danced gracefully, her feet tapping to the rhythm, and her smile beaming with pride. The audience cheered and clapped as she finished her routine.

After the recital, Susan felt a sense of accomplishment that she had never experienced before. She realized that her growth mindset had not only helped her become a better tap dancer but also a stronger and more resilient person. Her children and husband rushed to congratulate her, their faces filled with admiration and pride.

From that day forward, Susan's family saw her through a different lens—a lens of growth and possibility. They saw that age and skill level should never be barriers to pursuing one's dreams. Susan's journey to learn to tap dance not only transformed her but it also taught her family the invaluable lesson that with determination and a growth mindset, anything was possible. Susan had not only tapped her way into the world of dance but deeper into the hearts of her loved ones as well.

A growth mindset makes such a difference in the life of an unstoppable mom. If you do not live by a growth mindset, I highly suggest you focus on developing one. It will not only make a huge difference for you, but also for your children as they learn and grow, and face unexpected challenges.

The following are examples of ways you can demonstrate a growth mindset. After each example, you will find three specific actions you can take to model and strengthen your growth mindset. Read through them and choose at least one example that resonates with you. Then, try at least one of the actions for that example and see how it makes you feel. Remember, changing a mindset takes time and the more you practice, the easier it gets.

MINDSET #1 - CULTIVATING A GROWTH MINDSET

Fostering Confidence and Independence: With a growth mindset, you foster independence and confidence in your children. By encouraging your children to have a growth mindset, you teach your children that they have control over their own development and success. This understanding can empower them, foster their independence, and equip them with the confidence to navigate the world on their own terms.

- Encourage Decision-Making: Give your children opportunities to make decisions for themselves, even if they are small choices. This could involve letting them choose what to wear, what to eat, or how to spend their free time. Encouraging decision-making builds confidence in their ability to make choices and take responsibility for their choices.
- Provide Supportive Feedback: Offer positive and constructive feedback when your children take initiative or demonstrate independence. Acknowledge their efforts and achievements, and provide guidance when needed. This feedback reinforces their confidence in their abilities.
- Promote Problem-Solving: Encourage problem-solving skills by allowing your children to face and overcome challenges on their own, with guidance as necessary. This empowers them to find solutions independently and builds confidence in their problem-solving abilities.

Cultivating Resilience: With a growth mindset, you're cultivating resilience - in yourself and in your children. Life will inevitably present challenges and setbacks. By viewing these not as insurmountable obstacles but as opportunities for growth, you and your children will become more resilient and better equipped to handle whatever life throws your way.

- Practice Self-Care: Prioritize self-care activities such as exercise, meditation, and relaxation techniques. These practices help manage stress, boost emotional well-being, and build mental resilience.
- Learn from Setbacks: When facing challenges or setbacks, actively seek to learn from them. Reflect on what went wrong and what you can do differently next time. This learning mindset fosters resilience by turning adversity into growth opportunities.
- Seek Support: Reach out to a trusted friend, family member, or counselor when you're facing difficulties. Talking about your challenges and emotions with others can provide valuable perspective and emotional support, reinforcing your resilience.

<u>Embracing Challenges</u>: As a mom with a growth mindset, you don't shy away from challenges, whether they relate to parenting, personal growth, or professional development. You view difficulties as opportunities to learn and grow, rather than as insurmountable obstacles.
- Problem-Solving: When faced with a challenge, actively engage in problem-solving. Break down the issue into manageable steps, consider different solutions, and take action to address it.
- Positive Mindset: Approach challenges with a positive mindset, seeing them as opportunities for growth and learning rather than insurmountable obstacles.
- Seek Help: If your child is struggling with schoolwork, you don't give up but seek out resources and strategies to help them improve. You don't let your child believe "I can't do this" but instead, you teach your child that he or she can learn the skills needed to do almost anything.

<u>Learning from Mistakes</u>: Instead of seeing mistakes as failures, you view them as learning opportunities. If you lose your temper or mishandle a

situation with your child, you reflect on the situation, learn from it, and consider how you can respond differently next time.

- Reflection and Adaptation: Take time to reflect on a mistake and its consequences. Consider what went wrong and why. Self-reflection helps identify areas for improvement. After recognizing the mistake, adjust your approach or behavior accordingly. Use the lessons learned to make better decisions in the future.
- Open Communication: When appropriate, openly acknowledge a mistake to those affected by it. This fosters transparency, accountability, and trust, which can lead to better relationships and fewer repeated errors.
- Communicate About Mistakes: When your child fails a test or says something that makes a friend unhappy, talk with them about how they can learn from what happened and figure out what they can do to correct the situation or to do better the next time.

Celebrating Progress: You recognize and celebrate small improvements and progress, both in yourself and in your children. For instance, if your child is making slow progress in reading, you appreciate and praise their efforts rather than focusing solely on the end goal.

- Reward Yourself: Celebrate your progress by treating yourself to a small reward or indulging in something you enjoy. It can be as simple as a favorite snack or an evening of relaxation.
- Praise and Encouragement: When your children achieve milestones or make progress, offer genuine praise and encouragement. Let them know that their efforts and accomplishments are valued and appreciated.
- Special Treat or Activity: Celebrate your children's progress by planning a special treat or activity that they enjoy. It could be a trip to their favorite park, a movie night, or a small reward, like their

favorite dessert. This reinforces their sense of achievement and makes the progress memorable and enjoyable.

Openness to Feedback: You're open to constructive criticism and use it as a tool for improvement. If your partner suggests a different approach to managing a child's behavior, you consider the advice thoughtfully and discuss it instead of dismissing it defensively.
- Actively Seeking Input: Proactively ask for feedback from colleagues, peers, or mentors in your professional or personal life. For instance, you might ask a coworker for feedback on a project or seek input from a friend about your communication style.
- Listening Actively: When receiving feedback, practice active listening. Give the person your full attention, ask clarifying questions, and show appreciation for their input, even if it's critical. This demonstrates a willingness to understand and learn from others.
- Implementing Changes: Act on the feedback you receive by making concrete changes or improvements. Whether it's adjusting your work approach based on constructive criticism or making personal changes based on input from loved ones, taking action shows that you value and respect the feedback you receive.

Continuous Learning: As a mom with a growth mindset, you are a lifelong learner. You constantly seek new knowledge and skills, whether that's reading parenting books, attending workshops, or learning a new hobby. You model this love of learning for your children.
- Taking Professional Development Courses: Taking courses or attending workshops related to your career or industry is a form of continuous learning. This can include online courses, certifications, or in-person training to stay updated with the latest knowledge and skills.

MINDSET #1 - CULTIVATING A GROWTH MINDSET

- Language Learning: Learning a new language or improving your proficiency in a language you already know is a valuable form of continuous learning. You can achieve this through language courses, apps, or language exchange programs.
- Personal Growth and Hobbies: Pursuing personal interests and hobbies can be a form of continuous learning. Whether it's learning to play a musical instrument, practicing photography, or exploring new cooking techniques, engaging in activities you're passionate about allows for ongoing learning and skill development.

<u>Teaching a Growth Mindset to Your Children</u>: You encourage your children to adopt a growth mindset. You teach them that intelligence and talent are not fixed traits and that effort, practice, and perseverance can help them improve and achieve their goals.

- Embrace Challenges: Encourage your children to view challenges as opportunities for growth rather than obstacles. When they face a difficult task or encounter setbacks, remind them that it's okay to make mistakes and that these experiences help them learn and improve. Offer praise for their effort and perseverance, regardless of the outcome.
- Model a Growth Mindset: Children often learn by example, so it's essential to model a growth mindset yourself. Be open about your own challenges and how you approach them with a positive and resilient attitude. Share stories of your own learning experiences and emphasize the importance of continuous learning and self-improvement.
- Praise Effort and Strategies: Instead of praising inherent talent or abilities, focus your praise on your children's efforts and strategies. When they work hard, show determination, or use effective problem-solving techniques, acknowledge and commend these behaviors.

This reinforces the idea that effort and strategy lead to success and encourages them to persist in the face of challenges.

<u>Believing in Change</u>: When faced with adverse behaviors from your children, you believe in their capacity to change and grow. You focus on nurturing their potential and guiding their development, rather than labeling them based on their current behavior.

- Academic Improvement: When you believe in your child's ability to improve academically, you provide additional support and resources to help your child succeed. This might involve tutoring, personalized learning plans, or extra practice to enhance your child's skills and academic performance.
- Behavioral Growth: When you believe in your children's capacity for behavioral change you work with them to address challenging behaviors. You can implement positive reinforcement, teach problem-solving skills, and provide consistent guidance to help your children learn and grow, promoting more positive behavior.
- Friendship and Social Skills: Believing in your child's ability to develop positive social skills and build meaningful friendships is essential. Encouraging your children to communicate, resolve conflicts, and empathize with others fosters their social growth and reinforces the belief that they can develop healthy relationships.

<u>Persistence</u>: As a mom with a growth mindset, you keep going, even when things get tough. If your toddler is having a difficult time with potty training, you don't give up or label your child as 'incapable'. Instead, you persist, try different strategies, and remain patient, understanding that learning takes time.

- Pursuing Education: Returning to school to further your education while juggling family responsibilities demonstrates persistence.

Despite the challenges of balancing coursework and family life, you persist in your pursuit of knowledge and personal growth.
- Career Advancement: Striving for career advancement and taking on additional responsibilities at work exemplifies persistence. You consistently work toward your professional goals, overcoming obstacles and setbacks along the way.
- Teaching Life Skills: Patiently teaching your child essential life skills, such as cooking, budgeting, or time management shows persistence in your commitment to their development. You persist in imparting valuable knowledge that will benefit them throughout their lives.

<u>Flexibility in Approach</u>: If something isn't working, you don't hesitate to change your approach. You understand that there isn't a one-size-fits-all solution to every problem.
- Adapting to New Parenting Methods: Sometimes, as a parent, you need to be flexible in your approach. You realize that what works for one child may not work for another. So, you're open to trying new parenting methods and adjusting your strategies to meet each child's unique needs and personality.
- Navigating a Career Change: In your professional life, you embrace flexibility. You understand that the career path you envision might shift, and that's okay. You're open to exploring new opportunities, acquiring new skills, and even considering a career change if it aligns better with your evolving goals and interests.
- Adjusting to Life Transitions: Life can throw unexpected changes your way. Whether it's a move to a new city, a shift in family dynamics, or a health challenge, you show flexibility in adapting to these transitions. You learn to go with the flow, seek creative solutions, and stay resilient in the face of change.

Encourage Risk-Taking: You encourage your children to try new things and take calculated risks, helping them understand that making mistakes is part of learning and growing.

- Exploring New Hobbies: Encourage yourself to explore new hobbies. Whether it's taking up rock climbing, learning to play a musical instrument, or trying your hand at painting, embrace the thrill of the unknown and push your boundaries to discover new passions.
- Outdoor Adventures: Encourage your children to take risks in outdoor activities. Let them climb trees, explore hiking trails, or try out adventurous sports like rock climbing or kayaking with proper safety measures in place. Encouraging them to step out of their comfort zones in nature helps build confidence and resilience.
- Creative Expression: Support your children in taking creative risks. Encourage them to pursue artistic endeavors like painting, writing, or music where they can freely express themselves without fear of judgment. Emphasize that making mistakes is a natural part of the creative process and can lead to new discoveries and growth.

Acknowledge Struggles: You don't pretend that everything is easy or perfect. You're honest about your struggles and show your children that it's okay to find things difficult. This could involve sharing about a challenge at work and how you're working to overcome it, which helps your children see that everyone - even adults – has to work hard and struggle sometimes.

- Sharing Personal Stories: Share stories from your own life where you faced challenges and struggles. Talk about how you felt during those times and what you did to overcome them. This helps your children understand that it's normal to encounter difficulties and that they can learn and grow from these experiences.
- Parenting Challenges: Acknowledging the struggles of parenting

is essential. Whether it's dealing with sleepless nights, tantrums, or the demands of juggling work and family life, recognizing these difficulties helps parents support one another and seek solutions together.
- Academic Obstacles: In the realm of education, it's important to acknowledge the struggles your children face. Whether it's a challenging subject, test anxiety, or adjusting to remote learning, acknowledging these difficulties opens the door to seeking help and finding strategies for improvement.

<u>Promote the Value of Effort Over Results</u>: You place more emphasis on the effort put into a task than on the final outcome. If your child brings home a poor grade, you focus on their study habits and efforts, discussing how they could improve, rather than focusing solely on the disappointing grade.
- School Projects: When your children work on school projects, emphasize the importance of putting in their best effort rather than just aiming for the highest grade. Encourage them to learn and grow through the process of researching, planning, and presenting, regardless of the final score.
- Sports and Hobbies: Whether your children are involved in sports or pursuing hobbies like music or art, stress the value of effort over immediate results. Emphasize that improvement and enjoyment come from practice, dedication, and the journey of learning, not just winning or achieving perfection.
- Parenting Challenges: As a parent, remember that parenting is a journey, and it's the effort you put into nurturing and guiding your children that truly matters. Sometimes, the results may not be immediate or evident, but your consistent effort in providing love and support will make a lasting impact.

Cultivate Curiosity and Creativity: You encourage your children's curiosity and creativity, reinforcing the idea that they can constantly learn, grow, and see things from different perspectives. You might encourage your child to ask questions about the plants and animals they encounter, fostering an attitude of exploration and learning.

- Science Experiments: Encourage your children to conduct simple science experiments at home. Provide them with materials and instructions for hands-on learning. Let their curiosity guide them as they explore the wonders of chemistry, physics, or biology, sparking their interest in the world of science and discovery.
- Storytelling and Imagination: Foster creativity in your children through storytelling and imaginative play. Encourage them to create their own stories, characters, and worlds. Provide props and materials for them to bring their imaginative ideas to life, allowing them to explore their creativity freely.
- Artistic Expression: Embrace your creative side by experimenting with different forms of artistic expression. Try your hand at painting, drawing, writing, or music. Don't worry about perfection; let your curiosity guide you in exploring new techniques and styles. Allow your creativity to flow freely and see where it takes you.

Emotional Intelligence: You work on understanding and regulating your emotions, demonstrating to your children how to manage their own emotions effectively. You view emotional challenges as an opportunity for growth in emotional intelligence, both for yourself and your children.

- Empathy for Others: In your interactions with friends and colleagues, practice empathy by actively listening to their concerns and emotions. Put yourself in their shoes, trying to understand their perspective and feelings. This emotional intelligence will strengthen your relationships and support those around you.
- Teaching Empathy: Encourage your children to develop empathy by

discussing feelings and emotions. When reading a book together, ask them how they think the characters feel in different situations. This helps them recognize and understand emotions, fostering empathy for others.
- Conflict Resolution: Teach your children conflict resolution skills by modeling emotional intelligence. When they have disagreements with friends or siblings, guide them to express their feelings and listen to the other person's perspective. This promotes understanding and helps them manage conflicts more effectively.

The Unseen Benefits: As a mom with a growth mindset, you also encourage the same mindset in your family environment. This goes beyond the immediate and visible benefits. With a growth mindset, your children learn to embrace failure, enjoy effort, and persist in the face of adversity. This mindset can positively affect not just their schoolwork but also their hobbies, relationships, and ultimately, their happiness and life satisfaction.
- Unseen Benefits of Exercise: In your daily routine, you may not immediately notice the unseen benefits of exercise. Beyond the physical changes, regular physical activity reduces stress, enhances mood, and boosts cognitive function, supporting your overall well-being and your children's overall well-being.
- Learning Patience: Teach your children that even though they might not see it right away, learning to wait their turn in games or activities teaches them patience. This important skill will help them in many areas of life as they grow.
- Acts of Kindness: Encourage your children to understand that when they share their toys or help a friend in need, they might not always see immediate rewards. However, these acts of kindness create unseen benefits by strengthening their friendships and making them more caring and considerate individuals.

<u>Teaching the Value of Perseverance</u>: One of the most powerful lessons that comes from adopting a growth mindset is the value of perseverance. In a world that often seeks instant gratification, the lesson of sticking with a task - even (or especially) when it's difficult – is a valuable one. You teach your children that not everything will come easily, and that's okay. The important thing is not to give up.

- Overcoming Challenges: Encourage your children to persevere when facing challenges, whether it's a difficult school assignment or learning a new skill. Remind them that success often requires repeated efforts and the willingness to keep trying, even when things get tough.
- Setting Goals: Teach the importance of setting goals and working steadily toward them. Help your children understand that achieving their dreams may take time and effort. By consistently working toward their goals, they'll learn the value of perseverance and determination.
- Modeling Perseverance: Set an example by demonstrating perseverance in your own pursuits. Whether it's completing a long-term project, pursuing a hobby, or tackling personal challenges, your children will learn from your determination and commitment to seeing things through to the end.

***

Being a mom with a growth mindset is about being an unstoppable mother. It's about understanding that you and your children are capable of learning and growing, and about cultivating an environment that encourages this. With a growth mindset, you can make the journey of motherhood not just about raising children, but also about growing with them. This mindset can make your journey as a mother more fulfilling, more resilient, and yes, unstoppable.

Adopting a growth mindset doesn't mean you will never have moments of doubt or difficulty. But with this mindset, those moments become opportunities to learn, adapt, and grow stronger. Developing a growth mindset is a journey, and it's natural to occasionally lapse into a fixed mindset. The key is to recognize these moments and remind yourself of the power and potential of growth.

Chapter Summary

• **Fostering a Growth Mindset is Important:** Embrace a growth mindset in your motherhood journey, understanding that skills and abilities, including your own as a mother, can be developed through effort. This mindset helps you view challenges as learning opportunities rather than insurmountable obstacles.

• **Continue to Learn and Adapt:** Acknowledge the continuous learning and adaptation involved in being a mom. Allow yourself to make mistakes, learn from them, and evolve your parenting strategies as your children grow and change.

• **Create a Learning Environment for Your Child:** Apply a growth mindset to your child's development by creating an environment that encourages learning and exploration. Avoid labeling your child, and instead, focus on effort, perseverance, and strategy.

• **Face Challenges with Resilience:** When facing challenges, use a growth mindset to view these situations as opportunities for learning and growth. Adapt your strategies and learn new skills to effectively overcome any hurdles that slow you down.

• **Your Personal Growth Matters Too:** Recognize that your personal growth is essential and beneficial to both you and your children. Model lifelong learning and overcoming challenges to your children, demonstrating that growth extends beyond academic or professional areas.

• **The Impact of a Growth Mindset on Your Children:** Children raised in a growth mindset environment are more likely to develop resilience, confidence, adaptability, and a lifelong love of learning. This mindset equips them with essential skills for success in all areas of life.

- **Understand Your Journey:** Recognize that adopting a growth mindset is a continuous journey. It's normal to have moments of doubt or to occasionally revert to a fixed mindset. The key is to be aware of these moments and consciously redirect your thoughts towards growth and learning.

- **Three Practical Steps to Demonstrate a Growth Mindset:** Embrace the following three strategies to develop your growth mindset: look for learning opportunities, encourage effort over perfection, and model resilience.

Chapter 7

Mindset #2 - Harnessing Positivity
The Secret Ingredient of an Unstoppable Mom

> *"No influence is so powerful as that of the mother."*
> - Sarah Josepha Hale

Motherhood is a vibrant canvas, painted with hues of various experiences and emotions. Amidst this colorful mosaic, one trait stands out, often marking the difference between a challenging journey and a rewarding one. That trait is positivity.

An unstoppable mom strives to maintain a positive attitude, understanding the transformative power of positivity. While you allow yourself the authenticity to experience and express a range of emotions, you consciously avoid dwelling on negative feelings. Instead, you choose to celebrate small victories and practice gratitude, creating a nurturing and uplifting environment for yourself and your family.

For me, positivity is one of my most important mindsets. It lets me focus on the good in everything around me and see the light in all that I do. My cup is always half full and I share this philosophy with my children. My son Ben exemplifies a positive attitude. When things aren't going as he wants them to, he finds a way to see something good in what is happening. He is especially talented at guiding discussions with his siblings that helps them to see the good in almost any situation. My mother-in-law lives with us and sometimes there are frustrations expressed about things she says and does. Ben is always able to take the conversation and find something positive in what was said or done. It's a great skill to have. This is a mindset I truly WANT my children to model.

Maintaining a positive attitude does not mean ignoring the challenging aspects of motherhood or suppressing negative emotions. On the contrary, unstoppable moms like you validate and express their feelings, acknowledging that experiencing a range of emotions, including frustration, worry, or exhaustion, is part of the human experience. However, you avoid getting trapped in a cycle of negativity. You express your feelings, learn from the experience, and then shift your focus back to positivity.

You understand the potency of celebrating small victories. Whether it is your child successfully tying their shoes for the first time or overcoming a fear, or you managing to balance work and home successfully - you recognize and celebrate these moments. These celebrations do not have to be grand; a simple acknowledgment or a word of appreciation is often enough. This practice of recognizing small wins amplifies positivity, fostering a sense of accomplishment and encouraging continued effort and growth.

Positivity, however, is not just about your well-being. A positive attitude is contagious; it creates a warm and encouraging environment for your children too. Your children, in your presence, feel loved, accepted, and confident. They are more likely to develop a positive self-image, take on challenges, and exhibit optimism.

Moreover, your children look to you as a role model. When they see you embracing positivity, they learn to do the same. They learn to focus on their strengths, to see challenges as opportunities, and to appreciate the good in their lives. By practicing positivity, you not only enhance your own well-being but also significantly influence your children's outlook on life.

Positivity is a powerful cornerstone of unstoppable motherhood. By maintaining a positive attitude, celebrating small victories, and practicing gratitude, you can navigate the journey of motherhood with greater joy and satisfaction. You create a nurturing environment for your children and instill in them a positive outlook on life. While motherhood undeniably comes with its share of trials and tribulations, the beacon of positivity illuminates the path, transforming your journey into an enriching and fulfilling experience.

Gratitude is another powerful tool in an unstoppable mom's positivity box. By consciously acknowledging the blessings in your life, you can cultivate a positive outlook. This could be appreciation for your child's laughter, a supportive partner, a roof overhead, or even a quiet moment with a cup of coffee. Practicing gratitude helps shift your focus from problems and shortcomings to blessings and strengths, promoting positivity and contentment.

As an example of the impact a mom's positive outlook has on her children, let's take a look at a story about a mom named Jane:

While she loved her two children dearly, Jane tended to focus on the negative side of things rather than the positive. Her habit of seeing the glass as half-empty had a subtle but profound impact on her children's outlook on life.

One evening as Jane was preparing dinner in the kitchen, she overheard her youngest child, Lily, talking with her friend on the phone. Lily was discussing a recent school project, but all she seemed to mention were the challenges and difficulties she had faced. Jane couldn't help but listen intently, realizing that Lily was echoing her own habitual negative thinking.

Curiosity piqued, Jane approached Lily and asked, "Lily, why do you always talk about the tough parts of your schoolwork? What about the things that went well?"

Lily paused for a moment, then replied, "Well, that's what you always say, Mom. You usually talk about what's hard or what could go wrong."

Jane's heart sank as she realized the truth in Lily's words. She had unwittingly passed on her habit of negativity to her child. She felt like she had failed as a mother in that moment, but she also saw an opportunity for change.

Determined to break this pattern and set a better example for her children, Jane decided to transform her mindset. She started by consciously changing the way she framed her thoughts. Whenever a negative thought surfaced, she made an effort to find a positive aspect or a solution. It wasn't easy, but Jane was committed to making the change for herself and her children.

Slowly but steadily, Jane's mindset began to shift. She started to focus on the bright side of situations and encouraged her children to do the same. When they faced challenges, she'd say, "Yes, this is tough, but let's think about how we can overcome it." She made an effort to celebrate their achievements, no matter how small, and turned everyday occurrences into opportunities for gratitude.

Over time, Jane noticed a change not only in herself but also in her children. They began to adopt a more positive outlook on life. Her older child, Michael, started looking for solutions rather than dwelling on problems, and Lily began to express gratitude for the good things that happened each day.

One evening, as the family sat around the dinner table, Jane couldn't help but smile. She had transformed not only her own mindset but also the mindsets of her children. They now saw her as a source of positivity and inspiration, someone who had overcome her own negative tendencies to become a beacon of optimism.

As Jane looked at her children, she felt a profound sense of pride and accomplishment. She knew that by changing her mindset, she had not only improved her own life but had also given her children a valuable lesson in the power of positivity. From that day forward, the family's conversations were filled with optimism, hope, and a deep appreciation for the brighter side of life. Jane had successfully turned her home into a haven of positivity, and she cherished the newfound bond she shared with her children as they all embraced their more positive mindset together.

Positivity is a powerful tool that you can use to cultivate a healthy, happy environment for both yourself and your children. The following are examples of how you can harness a positive mindset. After each example, you will find three specific actions you can take to model and strengthen your positivity. Read through them and choose at least one example that resonates with you. Then, try at least one of the actions and see how it makes you feel. Remember, changing a mindset takes time and the more you practice, the easier it gets.

Affirmations: Use positive affirmations to boost your self-esteem and maintain a positive outlook. Phrases like "I am doing my best" or "I am a good mom" can be powerful reminders of your worth and efforts.

- Daily Affirmations: Set aside time each day to speak positive affirmations aloud to yourself. Repeatedly affirm your strengths, capabilities, and positive qualities. For example, say, "I am confident," "I am resilient," or "I am worthy of love and success."
- Mirror Work: Stand in front of a mirror and look into your own eyes while reciting positive affirmations. This direct eye contact reinforces the affirmations and helps build self-confidence. For example, say, "I love and accept myself unconditionally."
- Affirmation Journaling: Keep a journal where you write down positive affirmations. Reflect on your achievements, small victories, and positive qualities regularly. This practice reinforces a positive self-image and fosters self-belief.

Gratitude Practice: By acknowledging and expressing gratitude for the good things in your life, you can shift your focus from negative to positive. This could be through a gratitude journal, or simply taking a moment each day to reflect on what you're grateful for.

- Say "Thank You": The simplest and most direct way to show gratitude is by verbally expressing your thanks when someone does something kind or helpful for you.
- Write a Thank-You Note: A handwritten thank-you note or card can convey your appreciation in a thoughtful and personal way. It's especially effective for more formal occasions or when expressing gratitude to someone from a distance. Sadly, the act of writing thank you cards is becoming a rare occurrence. When was the last time you received or wrote a thank you card? What a great habit to teach your children!
- Acts of Kindness: Return the favor by performing acts of kindness for a person who helped you. This can create a positive cycle of giving and gratitude.

Modeling Positive Behavior: You can model positivity by handling challenges with optimism and grace. This can teach your children to approach difficulties in a similar way.

- Give Compliments: You can give sincere compliments to your child. Complimenting someone's efforts, appearance, or positive qualities can boost their self-esteem and create a positive atmosphere. It teaches the importance of acknowledging and appreciating the good in others.
- Volunteer Together: Engaging in volunteer work as a family can be a powerful way to model positive behavior. Whether it's helping at a local shelter, participating in a community cleanup, or volunteering for a charitable event, working together to give back to the community

fosters a sense of social responsibility and empathy.
- Share and Take Turns: Teach the importance of sharing and taking turns, not just with toys but also with responsibilities and opportunities. Whether it's sharing a toy with a sibling or taking turns to choose a family activity, this behavior reinforces cooperation, empathy, and fairness.

<u>Focusing on Strengths</u>: Instead of dwelling on weaknesses or mistakes, you can focus on your strengths and accomplishments, as well as those of your children. This can boost self-esteem and confidence for everyone in the family.
- Strengths-Based Conversations: Engage in conversations that highlight and celebrate each other's strengths and accomplishments. For moms, this means acknowledging and praising your child's abilities and achievements, whether in academics, sports, arts, or other areas. Encourage open discussions about what makes each family member unique and talented.
- Set and Celebrate Goals: Encourage setting goals that leverage individual strengths and interests. When setting goals, emphasize how a person's strengths can be utilized to achieve those goals. Celebrate progress and achievements along the way, reinforcing the idea that success is often built upon existing strengths.
- Skills Development: Focus on nurturing and developing existing strengths and talents rather than dwelling on weaknesses. Encourage your children to pursue activities and hobbies that align with their interests and natural abilities. Whether it's learning a musical instrument, joining a sports team, or pursuing an academic subject they excel in, investing in strengths can lead to increased confidence and fulfillment.

MINDSET #2 - HARNESSING POSITIVITY

<u>Cultivating Joy</u>: You can cultivate positivity by regularly engaging in activities that bring you joy, whether that's a hobby, spending time with friends, or simply taking a moment to enjoy a cup of tea.

- Practice Gratitude Daily: Take a few moments each day to reflect on and write down things you're grateful for. It could be as simple as appreciating a beautiful sunrise, a friendly interaction, or a delicious meal. Practicing gratitude helps shift your focus towards positive aspects of life and boosts feelings of joy. A discussion about what your children are grateful for at breakfast or during the drive to school is an excellent way to start the day on a positive note.
- Engage in Mindfulness and Meditation: Incorporate mindfulness and meditation into your daily routine. These practices encourage you to be fully present in the moment, letting go of worries and stress. By grounding yourself in the present, you can find joy in simple experiences, such as the sensation of a warm breeze or the taste of your favorite food.
- Pursue Passion Projects: Dedicate time to activities and hobbies that genuinely bring you joy and fulfillment. Whether it's painting, playing a musical instrument, gardening, or any other passion, allocating time to what you love can lead to a sense of purpose and happiness. Make it a priority to engage in these activities regularly.

<u>Positive Reinforcement</u>: You can use positive reinforcement to encourage good behavior in your children. By praising your children for their efforts and achievements, you can promote a positive, can-do attitude.

- Praise and Affirmation: Offer verbal praise and affirmations when your child exhibits a behavior or action you want to reinforce. Be specific in your compliments, highlighting the exact behavior or effort you appreciate. For example, if a child completes their homework on time, you can say, "I'm so proud of you for finishing your homework promptly. That shows great responsibility!"

- Reward Systems: Implement a reward system to reinforce positive behavior consistently. Create a chart or a system where your child can earn points, stickers, or tokens for accomplishing tasks or demonstrating desired behaviors. Once they accumulate a certain number of points, they can exchange them for a reward or privilege, such as extra playtime, a special treat, or a fun activity.
- Positive Feedback Loop: Encourage a positive feedback loop by acknowledging and reinforcing a series of connected positive behaviors. When your child starts a positive behavior, acknowledge it, and then point out how it leads to even more positive outcomes.

<u>Maintaining a Positive Environment</u>: You can foster a positive home environment by keeping things tidy, creating spaces for relaxation and creativity, and promoting open and positive communication.

- Family Meetings: Involve children in regular family meetings where everyone has a chance to express their thoughts, concerns, and ideas. Encourage open and respectful communication during these gatherings. This helps children feel heard and valued, contributing to a positive family environment. You can facilitate these meetings by setting aside dedicated time and actively listening to your children's input.
- Establish Clear Boundaries and Expectations: Clearly define and communicate family rules and expectations to children. Ensure that these rules are fair and age-appropriate. When boundaries are clear, children know what is expected of them. This reduces conflicts and promotes a sense of security. You play a crucial role in enforcing these boundaries consistently and providing guidance on why they are important.
- Self-Care for Moms: For moms, self-care is vital to maintaining a positive family environment. You are encouraged to take time for yourself, engage in activities you enjoy, and manage your stress

effectively. When you are well-rested and emotionally balanced, you can better support and nurture your children, contributing to a harmonious home.

Mindfulness: Through mindfulness, you can focus on the present moment, letting go of worries about the past or future. This can help cultivate a more positive and appreciative outlook.
- Mindful Breathing: Take a few moments to focus on your breath. Sit or stand comfortably, close your eyes, and take a slow, deep breath in through your nose, allowing your abdomen to rise. Exhale slowly through your mouth. Pay attention to the sensation of your breath and the rise and fall of your chest or abdomen. If your mind wanders, gently bring your focus back to your breath. This simple practice can help you become more grounded and centered.
- Mindful Walking: Take a walk in nature or around your neighborhood while paying full attention to the act of walking. Feel the ground beneath your feet, notice the movement of your body, and observe the sights and sounds around you. This practice can help you connect with the present moment and reduce stress.
- Mindful Journaling: Set aside time to journal your thoughts and feelings without judgment. Write about your experiences, emotions, and any insights you gain during your mindfulness practices. This can be a helpful tool for self-reflection and gaining a deeper understanding of your inner world.

Positive Self-Talk: You can harness positivity by being mindful of your internal dialogue. By challenging negative thoughts and replacing them with positive ones, you can maintain a more optimistic mindset.
- Internal Conversations: Make a conscious effort to be kind to yourself when engaging in discussions in your head. Become your own best

friend and remind yourself of the things you like about yourself. This is a skill your children can learn and benefit from too.

- Challenge Negative Thoughts: When you catch yourself thinking negatively about yourself, consciously challenge those thoughts. Ask yourself if there is evidence to support these negative beliefs or if they are based on assumptions or insecurities. Replace negative thoughts with more balanced and constructive ones. For example, if you think, "I'm terrible at this," challenge it with, "I may be facing a challenge, but I can learn and improve."
- Practice Self-Compassion: Treat yourself with the same kindness and understanding that you would offer to a friend. When you make a mistake or face a setback, avoid harsh self-criticism. Instead, acknowledge your imperfections and shortcomings with compassion. Remind yourself that everyone makes mistakes, and these experiences are opportunities for growth and learning.

Celebrating Small Wins: By acknowledging and celebrating small victories, you can keep a positive outlook and encourage persistence and resilience in the face of challenges. This could be as simple as congratulating your child for finishing a task or treating yourself for accomplishing a difficult task.

- Keep a Victory Journal: Record your small wins in a journal. Reflect on their significance to stay positive. Regularly reviewing your victory journal will serve as a reminder of your accomplishments and reinforce a positive outlook.
- Reward Yourself Thoughtfully: Celebrate victories with meaningful rewards aligned with your goals and values. By associating positive experiences with your achievements, you'll be more motivated to persist in the face of challenges. This reinforcement encourages resilience and a positive attitude.
- Share Success and Gratitude: Share your achievements with others

and express gratitude to reinforce resilience and positivity. Expressing gratitude for the progress you've made, and the people who support you can reinforce your positive outlook. Gratitude and sharing your successes with others can help you stay resilient and motivated.

<u>Visualizing Success</u>: When faced with a challenging situation, you can use visualization techniques to imagine a positive outcome. This can help reduce anxiety and encourage a more optimistic approach.

- Create a Vision Board: Compile images, words, and symbols that represent your goals and aspirations. Arrange them on a board or in a digital collage. Spend a few minutes each day looking at your vision board, imagining yourself achieving those goals.
- Mental Rehearsal: Close your eyes and vividly imagine yourself successfully accomplishing a specific task or achieving a goal. Visualize the process, including the challenges you might encounter and how you'll overcome them. This mental rehearsal can boost your confidence and preparedness.
- Set Specific Goals: Define clear and specific goals for yourself. Write them down with detailed descriptions of what success looks like. Regularly review your goals, reminding yourself of the desired outcome. This helps keep your focus on your objectives and reinforces the visualization of success.

<u>Setting Positive Goals</u>: By setting realistic, positive goals for yourself and your children, you can foster a sense of purpose and forward momentum.

- Goal Jar: Have your child decorate a jar and label it as their "Goal Jar." Write down achievable goals on small pieces of paper and place them in the jar. These goals can be related to school, hobbies, or personal growth. Periodically, sit down together to review your goals and celebrate your achievements.

- SMART Goals: Learn about SMART goals, where goals are Specific, Measurable, Achievable, Relevant, and Time-bound. Have your child set a SMART goal, such as improving their math grades by one letter grade within the next three months. Break down the goal into smaller, actionable steps to work on consistently.
- Personal Development Plan: Create a personal development plan that outlines your goals and aspirations. This plan can encompass various aspects of your life, such as career, health, relationships, or hobbies. Each goal should be specific, with a clear timeline and actionable steps. By setting and pursuing your own positive goals, you model goal-setting behavior for your child and demonstrate the importance of self-improvement.

Seeking Positive Influences: Surround yourself with positive influences—people who uplift you and encourage a positive outlook. This can include friends, family, or even positive influences found in books or online.

- Carefully Choose Your Social Media Feeds: Go through your social media accounts and unfollow or mute accounts that consistently share negative or toxic content. Seek out and follow accounts that promote positivity, inspiration, and personal growth. This simple action can significantly impact your daily mindset.
- Join Supportive Communities: Look for local or online communities that align with your interests and values. Whether it's a hobby club, a fitness group, or a support network, being part of positive and like-minded communities can provide encouragement, inspiration, and a sense of belonging.
- Uplifting Books or Articles: Regularly consume content that uplifts and inspires you. Whether it's motivational books, articles, or podcasts, exposing yourself to positive and empowering information can influence your thoughts, attitudes, and actions in a beneficial way.

MINDSET #2 - HARNESSING POSITIVITY

<u>Making Time for Fun</u>: Regularly scheduling time for enjoyable activities can help cultivate positivity. This could be a family game night, a date night, or simply time spent reading a good book.

- Schedule "Me Time": Set aside a specific time in your weekly schedule for your own leisure and enjoyment. It could be an hour to read a book, take a relaxing bath, or pursue a hobby you love. This action ensures that you prioritize self-care and fun amidst your responsibilities.
- Create a "Fun Day": Dedicate one day each month as a "Fun Day" for you and your child. On this day, engage in activities that both of you enjoy, whether it's playing board games, going to the park, or baking together. Make it a special occasion to bond and have fun.
- Plan Mini Adventures: Encourage your child to plan mini-adventures within your daily routine. For example, they can create a "treasure hunt" around the house, explore a new hiking trail, or have a picnic in the backyard. These small adventures add an element of excitement and fun to their everyday life.

<u>Practicing Kindness</u>: Acts of kindness, both to yourself and others, can foster a sense of positivity and well-being. This could be treating yourself to a favorite treat or doing something nice for a friend, neighbor, or family member.

- Compliment Someone: Take a moment to genuinely compliment someone on their appearance, achievements, or actions. A kind and sincere compliment can brighten someone's day and foster positivity. Giving a compliment can also brighten your day or your children's day.
- Random Acts of Kindness: Perform a random act of kindness for someone, such as holding the door open, helping with groceries, or leaving a friendly note. These small gestures can make a big difference in someone's life – and in your own.

- Listen Actively: When your child is speaking to you, practice active listening. Give them your full attention, maintain eye contact, and avoid interrupting. Show empathy and understanding in your responses. This demonstrates kindness through respectful communication.

Maintaining a Healthy Lifestyle: Regular exercise, a balanced diet, and sufficient sleep can all contribute to overall well-being and a more positive mood.
- Regular Exercise: Incorporate regular physical activity into your routine. Aim for at least 150 minutes of moderate-intensity aerobic exercise or 75 minutes of vigorous-intensity exercise per week, as recommended by health guidelines. Find activities you enjoy, such as walking, cycling, swimming, or dancing, to make exercise a sustainable habit.
- Balanced Nutrition: Focus on a balanced and nutritious diet. Include a variety of fruits, vegetables, whole grains, lean proteins, and healthy fats in your meals. Limit the consumption of processed foods, sugary drinks, and excessive amounts of salt. Pay attention to portion sizes and stay hydrated by drinking plenty of water.
- Prioritize Sleep: Ensure you get enough quality sleep each night. Most adults need 7-9 hours of sleep for optimal health. Create a sleep-friendly environment by keeping your bedroom dark, quiet, and cool. Establish a regular sleep schedule by going to bed and waking up at the same time each day to regulate your body's internal clock.

Finding Humor: Laughter truly can be the best medicine. Finding humor in everyday situations can lighten the mood and foster a positive, cheerful atmosphere at home.
- Share Funny Stories or Jokes: Share funny stories or jokes with your child, friends, family, or coworkers. Engaging in lighthearted

conversations and humor can create positive social interactions and boost your mood.
- Watch Comedy: Set aside time to watch a comedy movie, TV show, or stand-up comedy performance. Laughter is contagious, and enjoying humor through entertainment can provide a great opportunity to relax and unwind. Ever watched America's Funniest Home Videos? This show is guaranteed to put a smile on your face and your children's faces too!
- Find the Silver Lining: Train yourself to find the silver lining in challenging situations. When faced with adversity, try to see the humor or absurdity in the moment. This can help you cope with stress and view difficulties with a more positive perspective.

Embracing Change: Instead of resisting change, accepting and even embracing it can lead to a more positive outlook. This could apply to changes in routines, children growing up, or unexpected life events.
- Set an Example: You can lead by example and openly discuss your own experiences with change. Share personal stories of how you've adapted to new situations, whether it's a career change, moving to a new place, or learning a new skill. Your willingness to embrace change can inspire your child.
- Encourage Exploration: Encourage your child to explore new activities, hobbies, or interests. Be supportive when they express curiosity about trying something different. Reinforce the idea that change and growth often come from trying new things and stepping out of their comfort zone.
- Positive Mantras: Repeating positive mantras or quotes can help keep a positive perspective during challenging times. These could be phrases like "This too shall pass" or "Every day may not be good, but there is something good in every day."

<u>Practicing Forgiveness</u>: Holding onto anger or resentment can breed negativity. By practicing forgiveness, both towards yourself and others, you can let go of negative feelings and cultivate a more positive, peaceful outlook.

- Express Your Feelings: Start by acknowledging your own feelings and emotions related to the situation. It's essential to process your anger, hurt, or disappointment. Share these feelings with a trusted friend or therapist to gain perspective and emotional support.
- Empathize with the Other Person: Try to understand the other person's perspective and feelings. Consider the reasons behind their actions and whether they may have been influenced by their own challenges or struggles. Empathy can help you see the situation from a more compassionate standpoint.
- Choose to Forgive: Forgiveness is a conscious choice. Decide to let go of resentment, anger, and the desire for revenge. You don't have to forget, condone, or reconcile with the person, but you can release the negative emotions associated with the offense. This process can be liberating and promote personal growth. Being able to forgive others and move on is a skill that will benefit your children again and again.

***

Harnessing positivity is not about denying or suppressing negative emotions, but about consciously cultivating a positive perspective and mindset. It's a practice that takes time and patience, and it's okay to have bad days. The goal is to try and maintain an overall positive attitude. It's about approaching challenges with a can-do attitude, focusing on the good, and cultivating an environment of optimism and resilience.

Chapter Summary

- **Embrace Positivity:** Recognize the importance of maintaining a positive attitude in your motherhood journey. While it's essential to acknowledge and express a range of emotions, focus on steering away from prolonged negativity.

- **Show Authenticity in Your Emotions:** As an unstoppable mom, validate and express your feelings, understanding that experiencing frustration, worry, or exhaustion is natural. However, avoid dwelling in negativity and learn to shift back to positivity.

- **Celebrate Small Victories:** Acknowledge and celebrate small accomplishments, whether they're your child's or your own. Recognizing these moments amplifies positivity and fosters a sense of achievement and growth.

- **Practice Gratitude:** Cultivate a habit of gratitude. Regularly acknowledge the blessings in your life, whether they're big or small. This practice helps shift your focus from problems to positivity and contentment.

- **Create a Positive Environment for Your Family:** Your positive attitude influences the atmosphere of your home. It creates a nurturing and encouraging environment, helping your children to feel loved, accepted, and confident.

- **Role Model Positivity for Children:** Children learn from your example. When they see you embracing positivity, they are more likely to develop a positive self-image, approach challenges optimistically, and appreciate the good in their lives.

- **Harness Positivity as a Tool for Fulfillment:** Use positivity as a powerful tool to navigate the journey of motherhood with joy and satisfaction. Positivity transforms challenges into enriching experiences and creates a healthy, happy environment for both you and your children.

- **Cultivating Positivity Takes Time and Patience:** Remember that harnessing positivity is a practice that requires time and patience. It's okay to have difficult days. The goal is to maintain an overall positive attitude, focusing on the good and build resilience.

Chapter 8

Mindset #3 - Patience and Understanding
The Pillars of an Unstoppable Mom

"It's not until you become a mother that your judgment slowly turns to compassion and understanding."
- Erma Bombeck

Motherhood is often described as a journey of profound love, accompanied by a myriad of challenges, learning opportunities, and transformative experiences. Two paramount qualities guiding this journey are patience and understanding. Unstoppable moms practice these virtues not only with their children but also with themselves. Recognizing the inherent imperfection in all humans, they appreciate that everyone, including themselves and their children, will make mistakes. Rather than letting frustration overshadow these moments, they use these instances as opportunities for growth and learning.

Patience is a remarkable virtue, especially in the context of motherhood. Children are in a constant state of learning and growth, which means they will inevitably make mistakes, test boundaries, and sometimes behave in ways that challenge your patience. Unstoppable moms understand this, responding with calmness and patience, and giving their children the space to learn from their mistakes and experiences. Instead of rushing to correct, they allow the natural consequences to unfold, thereby fostering a learning environment that encourages self-correction and independence.

Understanding complements patience in unstoppable motherhood. Your understanding nurtures a sense of empathy, enabling you to see the world through your child's eyes. This perspective allows you to decipher the underlying needs or emotions driving your child's behavior, helping you to respond in a more supportive and effective manner. For instance, when their child throws a tantrum, instead of reacting with frustration, an understanding mother seeks to identify the root cause - be it tiredness, hunger, or over stimulation - and addresses that need.

Patience and understanding should not only be extended to children but also to yourself. Motherhood is a challenging role, and even the most unstoppable moms are not immune to mistakes. They may lose their patience, misjudge a situation, or struggle to balance their various roles and responsibilities. It is crucial in these moments for moms to show themselves the same patience and understanding they offer their children. By acknowledging their fallibility and treating themselves with compassion, moms can learn from their missteps without succumbing to guilt or self-criticism.

Treating mistakes as teachable moments, both for yourself and your children, is a powerful practice that unstoppable moms adopt. Rather than viewing mistakes as failures, they perceive them as opportunities for growth. Every mishap is a chance to learn something new, to improve, and to demonstrate how to handle mistakes with grace and resilience. This approach not only enhances your personal growth but also imparts essential life skills to your children.

How many times have you done something that you wish you hadn't done and you just beat yourself up for it? You keep going over what happened in your mind and each time you do, you feel the same frustration or anger or impatience you felt when the event first happened. I have done this more times than I want to remember. Thankfully, I learned an effective strategy to show myself some grace and understanding - I stop those conversations in my head as soon as they begin. I make a conscious effort to change the discussion in my mind so I move away from the thought I do not like to one that is much more positive and uplifting. It is amazing how much this strategy can help you. When you remove negative, frustrating, impatient and angry discussions from your mind and replace them with more positive thoughts, your whole being is beneficially affected

Patience and understanding are essential guiding lights in the voyage of motherhood. Together, they allow you to navigate your children's growth and your own journey with empathy, resilience, and grace. By practicing patience and understanding, you foster an environment of love and learning, transforming the challenges of motherhood into opportunities for growth. In this nurturing atmosphere, children flourish, and mothers evolve, turning the rich tapestry of motherhood into a beautiful work of enduring love and shared growth.

As an example of the impact a mom has when she shows her children patience and understanding, lets take a look at a story about a mom named Meredith:

Meredith was a dedicated mother to two energetic children. While she loved her family deeply, she struggled with patience and understanding. Her days often felt like a whirlwind of chaos, and she found herself losing her temper and snapping at her children more often than she'd like.

One evening, as Meredith tucked her kids into bed, her youngest, Emily, asked, "Mom, why do you get so mad sometimes?" It was a simple question, but it hit Meredith like a bolt of lightning. She realized that her impatience was affecting her children more than she had thought.

Meredith decided it was time for a change. She knew she needed to work on her patience and understanding to create a more peaceful and loving atmosphere at home. She started by taking a deep breath whenever she felt frustration welling up. She would remind herself that her children were learning and growing, and mistakes were a part of that process.

As Meredith continued her journey to become a more patient and understanding mother, she also noticed a positive shift in her relationship with her partner, Tom. She found herself listening more attentively when he shared his thoughts and concerns, and she responded with empathy rather than frustration. This newfound patience and understanding brought them closer together, making their partnership stronger.

But the changes didn't stop there. Meredith's transformation spilled over into her workplace. She realized that practicing patience and understanding wasn't just beneficial at home; it could also improve her interactions with coworkers. She began to actively listen to her colleagues during meetings and considered their perspectives before responding. This change in attitude led to better teamwork and more harmonious working relationships.

Over time, Meredith became known not only as a loving and patient mother at home but also as a supportive and understanding colleague at work. She had discovered that the power of patience and understanding extended far beyond her family and had a positive impact on every aspect of her life.

One day, as Meredith watched her children play together peacefully, she couldn't help but smile. She had come a long way on her journey to becoming a more patient and understanding mom, partner, and coworker. Her children now saw her as a source of comfort and guidance, and her relationship with Tom had never been better.

Meredith's transformation had taught her that patience and understanding were not just virtues; they were keys to building stronger relationships and creating a more harmonious and joyful life. She felt grateful for the change she had made and looked forward to the future with a heart full of patience, understanding, and love.

Patience and understanding help to create a loving, secure, and supportive environment for children. The following are examples of how you can demonstrate patience and understanding. After each example, you will find three specific actions you can take to model and strengthen your patience and understanding mindset. Read through them and choose at least one example that resonates with you. Then, try at least one of the actions and see how it makes you feel. Remember, changing a mindset takes time and the more you practice, the easier it gets.

<u>Coping with Tantrums</u>: When your child, especially toddlers, throws tantrums over seemingly minor issues, it's important to acknowledge their feelings, stay calm, and wait out the tantrum. Explain gently why certain behaviors are unacceptable.

- Stay Calm and Patient: When your child has a tantrum, it's important for you to remain calm and patient. Take deep breaths to manage your own emotions and avoid reacting with frustration or anger. Remember that tantrums are a normal part of child development, and your calm demeanor can help de-escalate the situation.
- Use Positive Reinforcement: Encourage positive behavior by offering praise and rewards for appropriate actions and self-control. Reinforce good behavior by acknowledging and appreciating it. For example, if your child calms down after a tantrum, say, "Thank you for calming down and using your words to tell me what you need. That's very helpful."
- Provide a Safe Space: If possible, move your child to a quiet and safe space where they can express their emotions without harm. Stay with them to offer support and comfort, but avoid engaging in arguments or negotiations during the tantrum. Once the tantrum subsides, you can talk about the situation and help your child identify their feelings and needs.

MINDSET #3 - PATIENCE AND UNDERSTANDING

<u>Handling Sibling Rivalry</u>: It takes patience to mediate between squabbling siblings and understand each child's perspective. Take the time to listen to each child and guide them towards resolving their conflicts amicably.

- Promote Individual Quality Time: Spend one-on-one time with each child separately. Engage in activities that cater to their interests and needs. This individual attention helps children feel valued and reduces the need to compete for your attention.
- Teach Conflict Resolution: Encourage siblings to express their feelings and concerns openly and calmly. Teach them effective communication and conflict resolution skills, such as active listening, using "I" statements, and finding compromises. Act as a mediator when needed but also empower them to resolve disputes independently when appropriate.
- Foster a Sense of Teamwork: Encourage collaboration and teamwork among siblings. Assign them shared responsibilities or tasks that require cooperation, such as cleaning up together, preparing a meal, or working on a project. Emphasize that they are a team and can achieve more when they work together than when they compete against each other.

<u>Supporting Slow Learners</u>: If your child is struggling academically, take the time to help with homework, learn the areas where your child is struggling, and find different ways to explain or approach the problem.

- Tailored Learning Plans: Work with educators to create a personalized learning plan for your child. This plan should take into account their specific strengths, weaknesses, and learning style. It may involve additional tutoring, modified assignments, or extended time for assessments to ensure they have the opportunity to grasp and master concepts at their own pace.
- Regular Progress Monitoring: Keep track of your child's progress and celebrate their achievements, no matter how small. Regularly

review their schoolwork, assignments, and test results to identify areas where they may need extra help or attention. Provide positive feedback and encouragement to boost their confidence.
- Supportive Environment: Create a supportive and nurturing environment at home. Encourage open communication, and let your child know that it's okay to ask questions and seek help when needed. Foster a love for learning by engaging in educational activities together, visiting libraries, and exploring their interests outside of the classroom.

<u>Managing Teen Rebellion</u>: The teenage years can be fraught with rebellion and emotional upheaval. Understand this phase of development and provide guidance, maintain boundaries, but also give space for your teenager to grow and learn from their mistakes.
- Open Communication: Maintain open and non-judgmental communication with your teenager. Encourage them to express their thoughts, feelings, and concerns without fear of punishment or criticism. Listen actively, validate their emotions, and try to understand their perspective. This helps build trust and fosters a positive connection.
- Set Clear Boundaries and Expectations: Establish clear and reasonable boundaries and expectations for your teenager's behavior, both at home and in their social life. Ensure that consequences for breaking these boundaries are fair and consistent. Explain the reasons behind the rules and boundaries, emphasizing safety and respect for others.
- Offer Independence and Responsibility: Gradually allow your teenager more independence and decision-making power in their life. This can include responsibilities like managing their own schedule, chores, or budgeting. By giving them opportunities to make choices and learn from their mistakes in a controlled environment, you empower them to become responsible and accountable adults.

MINDSET #3 - PATIENCE AND UNDERSTANDING

Dealing with Fussy Eaters: Many children go through phases of being fussy eaters. Understand and be patient with your child, gradually introduce new foods, respect dislikes, and create a stress-free eating environment, rather than forcing them to eat something they don't want.

- Offer a Variety of Foods: Introduce a wide range of foods to your fussy eater's diet. Include different fruits, vegetables, proteins, and grains. Make meals colorful and visually appealing. Encourage them to try new foods by incorporating them into dishes they already enjoy or by offering small tastes as a sample.
- Involve Them in Meal Preparation: Include your fussy eater in meal preparation activities. Let them help wash, chop, or mix ingredients. When children are involved in the cooking process, they often become more curious about the foods they are preparing and are more likely to try them.
- Maintain a Positive Mealtime Environment: Create a positive and stress-free mealtime environment. Avoid pressuring or bribing your child to eat. Instead, focus on pleasant and relaxed family meals where everyone sits together and enjoys each other's company. Limit distractions like TV or devices during mealtime to encourage mindful eating.

Teaching New Skills: Whether it's tying shoelaces, riding a bike, or learning to read, children require patient instruction and encouragement. Understand that each child learns at their own pace and provide gentle, consistent guidance.

- Break Down the Skill: Divide the skill into smaller, manageable steps or tasks. This makes it easier for your child to understand and practice. For example, if you're teaching them to tie their shoes, start with teaching them how to make a simple knot before moving on to the full shoelace bow.
- Demonstrate and Guide: Show your child how to perform the skill

through clear and patient demonstrations. Then, guide them as they practice. Offer constructive feedback and encouragement as they build their confidence. Be patient, as learning new skills may require repeated attempts.

- Provide Resources and Practice: Offer resources and tools that support the learning process. This could include books, online tutorials, or age-appropriate equipment. Encourage your child to practice regularly, and create a positive and supportive environment where they feel comfortable making mistakes and learning from them.

Understanding Unique Personalities: Each child has their own personality, quirks, and ways of expressing themselves. Appreciate your child's individuality, even when it's vastly different from your own or from societal expectations.

- Active Listening: Practice active listening when engaging with your child. Give your full attention to what they're saying without interrupting or judging. Ask open-ended questions to encourage them to express themselves. By actively listening, you can gain insights into their thoughts, feelings, and perspectives, allowing you to better understand their unique personality.
- Empathize and Validate: Show empathy and validation towards your child's emotions and experiences. Understand that your child may have different reactions and sensitivities due to their unique personality. Validate their feelings by acknowledging them and expressing understanding. This helps create a supportive and empathetic atmosphere.
- Respect Individual Differences: Recognize and respect the diversity of personalities and preferences among people. Avoid making assumptions or imposing your own expectations on your child based on your personality or beliefs. Instead, embrace the richness of

unique perspectives and approaches to life, and be open to learning from each other.

Navigating Emotional Ups and Downs: Children often don't fully understand their emotions and may express them in ways that seem disproportionate. Help your child navigate their emotions, providing comfort and helping them to understand and express their feelings in a healthy way.
- Emotion Validation: Teach your child that it's okay to have and express a wide range of emotions. Encourage them to talk about their feelings, whether positive or negative, without judgment. Let them know that all emotions are valid and that it's healthy to express and process them.
- Emotion Regulation Techniques: Teach your child age-appropriate emotion regulation techniques. This could include deep breathing exercises, counting to ten when upset, or using a feelings chart to help identify and label their emotions. Practicing these techniques can empower them to manage emotional highs and lows more effectively.
- Problem-Solving Skills: Guide your child in developing problem-solving skills when faced with emotional challenges. Help them identify the source of their emotions and brainstorm constructive solutions. Encourage them to think about the consequences of their actions and choose responses that align with their values and goals.

Accepting Mistakes: Children are bound to make mistakes. Don't scold immediately or jump to conclusions. Instead, take time to understand the situation and help your child see the learning opportunity in the mistake.
- Self-Reflection and Ownership: Encourage self-reflection when a mistake is made. Ask questions like, "What went wrong?" and "What

could we have done differently?" Take ownership of the mistake by acknowledging your role in it. Avoid blaming others or external factors.
- Learn and Adapt: View mistakes as valuable learning opportunities. Identify the lessons and insights that can be gained from the mistake. Use this newfound knowledge to make improvements and avoid repeating the same error in the future. Emphasize the idea that making mistakes is a natural part of the learning process.
- Practice Self-Compassion: Be kind and compassionate toward yourself when you make a mistake. Avoid harsh self-criticism or negative self-talk. Treat yourself with the same understanding and forgiveness that you would offer to a friend who made a mistake. This self-compassion fosters a healthy and positive mindset.

<u>Dealing with Changes in Routine</u>: Children may often disrupt daily routines, whether it's not wanting to go to bed, stalling before school, or delaying meals. Stay calm and explain the importance of routines, but also stay flexible to occasional changes.
- Plan and Communicate: When you anticipate a change in your routine, take time to plan for it. Communicate the change to those affected by it, whether it's your family, coworkers, or yourself. Clearly explain the reasons for the change and outline the new schedule or expectations. This proactive approach can reduce anxiety and confusion.
- Flexibility and Adaptation: Develop flexibility in your mindset and daily habits. Embrace change as an opportunity for growth and new experiences. When a change occurs, focus on adapting to the new circumstances rather than resisting them. Keep an open mind and be willing to adjust your expectations and plans accordingly.
- Self-Care and Stress Management: Recognize that changes in routine can sometimes lead to stress and anxiety. Prioritize self-care practices like mindfulness, meditation, physical activity, or

relaxation techniques to manage stress and maintain emotional well-being during transitions. Taking care of your mental and physical health can help you better cope with routine changes.

<u>Understanding and Responding to a Child's Fears</u>: Children have unique fears, some of which may seem irrational to adults. Listen to your child's fears, understand their perspective, and help them cope, instead of dismissing their feelings outright.

- Active Listening and Validation: When your child expresses fear, actively listen to their concerns without judgment or dismissal. Allow them to share their feelings and thoughts openly. Validate their emotions by acknowledging that it's okay to feel scared or anxious. Use phrases like, "I understand that you're feeling scared, and that's completely normal."
- Provide Reassurance: Offer reassurance and comfort to your child. Explain that you are there to keep them safe and protect them. Reassure them that their feelings are valid but that you will help them manage their fears. Depending on the fear, you might say, "I'm here with you, and I'll make sure you're safe," or "We can work through this together."
- Gradual Exposure and Education: For persistent or specific fears, educate your child about what they are afraid of and why it's not as frightening as it seems. Gradually expose them to the fear in a controlled and supportive manner. For example, if a child is afraid of dogs, start with friendly, well-trained dogs in a safe environment and gradually increase exposure as their comfort level grows.

<u>Encouraging Independence</u>: It requires patience to allow children to do things on their own, especially when they are slower or less proficient than adults. Allow your child to take the time they need to learn new tasks and become self-reliant, offering guidance only when necessary.

- Provide Age-Appropriate Responsibilities: Assign age-appropriate tasks and responsibilities to your child based on their abilities and maturity. This might include tasks like making their bed, setting the table, or packing their school bag. Gradually increase the complexity of their responsibilities as they grow and develop.
- Offer Choices and Decision-Making: Give your child opportunities to make choices and decisions within reasonable boundaries. For example, allow them to choose their outfits, select their after school activities, or pick a meal from a healthy menu. Encouraging them to make decisions fosters a sense of autonomy and responsibility.
- Support Problem-Solving: When your child faces challenges or problems, guide them through the process of finding solutions independently. Ask open-ended questions to help them think critically and consider different options. Encourage them to brainstorm solutions and make decisions, even if it means making mistakes along the way.

<u>Handling Health Issues</u>: Dealing with a sick child or managing chronic health issues requires patience and understanding. Stay calm during doctor's visits, handle medication schedules, and comfort a child who might not fully understand what they're going through.
- Seek Medical Advice: If your child is feeling sick and needs doctor intervention, consult with a healthcare professional. Reach out to your pediatrician or a healthcare provider for guidance and assessment. Describe your child's symptoms and any changes in their condition accurately. Follow the healthcare provider's recommendations for treatment, whether it involves medication, rest, or further evaluation.
- Provide Comfort and Support: Offer emotional and physical comfort to your sick child. Keep them hydrated, provide nutritious food when they're able to eat and ensure they get enough rest. Stay with them

to offer reassurance, read stories, or watch their favorite shows. A comforting and supportive presence can help alleviate their anxiety and discomfort.
- Monitor Symptoms: Keep a close eye on your child's symptoms and overall well-being. Document any changes in their condition, such as fever, cough, or other symptoms. Follow the prescribed medication or treatment plan diligently. If you notice worsening symptoms or new concerns, contact your healthcare provider for further guidance.

<u>Managing Sleep Issues</u>: Many children struggle with sleep issues, from nightmares to bed wetting, to resisting bedtime. Be patient and understanding, reassure your child, and try different strategies to help them overcome these challenges, understanding that this is a normal part of child development.
- Establish a Consistent Bedtime Routine: Create a consistent and calming bedtime routine that helps signal to your child that it's time to wind down and sleep. This routine might include activities like reading a book, taking a warm bath, or practicing relaxation exercises. Consistency is key, so aim to follow the routine at the same time each night.
- Create a Comfortable Sleep Environment: Ensure that your child's sleep environment is conducive to rest. This means keeping the bedroom dark, quiet, and at a comfortable temperature. Provide a comfortable mattress and bedding. If your child has specific sleep preferences, accommodate them as much as possible to create a reassuring sleep environment.
- Address Nighttime Fears and Anxiety: Many children experience nighttime fears or anxiety that can disrupt their sleep. Listen to your child's concerns and offer reassurance. A nightlight or a security object, like a favorite stuffed animal, can provide comfort. Encourage

your child to express their feelings and discuss any worries during the day rather than right before bedtime.

<u>Balancing Personal Time and Parenting</u>: Moms also need time for themselves, to pursue hobbies, work, or simply rest. Sometimes, children might not understand this need. Explain this to your children in a way they can understand, instilling respect for personal space and time in them.

- Establish a Schedule: Create a schedule or routine that includes dedicated blocks of personal time. Having a clear schedule helps ensure that you have a regular time set aside for yourself.
- Seek Support: Utilize your support network, such as family members, friends, or babysitters, to help with childcare when needed. This allows you to have regular breaks and personal time without compromising your child's well-being. Don't hesitate to ask for help when you need it.
- Prioritize Self-Care: Recognize the importance of self-care. Make self-care a non-negotiable part of your routine. Whether it's exercising, pursuing hobbies, or simply relaxing - taking care of your own physical and emotional needs helps you recharge and be more present when you're with your child.

***

Patience and understanding aren't about letting children do whatever they want. They are about providing a supportive environment where your children can grow, learn, and understand the consequences of their actions. Even the most patient and understanding mom can have moments of frustration. What matters is how you handle these moments and the overall consistent message of love, patience, and understanding that you communicate to your children.

Chapter Summary

• **Embrace Patience and Understanding:** Understand that patience and understanding are key virtues for a mom, guiding you through challenges and transformative experiences. Practice these qualities with your children and equally with yourself.

• **Patience is a Key Virtue:** Recognize the importance of patience, especially as children are constantly learning and growing. Respond to mistakes and challenging behaviors with calmness, allowing children to learn from natural consequences and develop independence.

• **Understanding Complements Patience:** Use understanding to nurture empathy, helping you see situations from your child's perspective. This approach allows for a more supportive and effective response to your child's needs and behaviors.

• **Have Self-Compassion for Yourself:** Extend the same patience and understanding to yourself as a mother. Acknowledge that mistakes are part of the parenting journey and treat yourself with compassion, avoiding guilt or self-criticism.

• **See Mistakes as Teachable Moments:** View mistakes, both yours and your children's, as opportunities for growth. Treat mishaps as chances to learn and demonstrate how to handle challenges with resilience and grace.

• **Foster a Supportive Environment:** By practicing patience and understanding, you create a loving, secure, and supportive environment for your children. This atmosphere promotes healthy development and helps children flourish.

- **Balance Your Guidance and Support:** Understand that patience and understanding do not mean allowing children to do whatever they want. They are about providing a supportive environment where children can learn from their actions and understand the consequences.

- **Recognize You Will Still Have Moments of Frustration:** Acknowledge that even the most patient and understanding moms can experience frustration. The key is how these moments are handled and ensuring that the overall message to your children is one of love, patience, and understanding.

Chapter 9

Mindset #4 - Unconditional Love
The Compass of an Unstoppable Mom

"If you want to change the world, go home and love your family."
– Mother Teresa

At the heart of unstoppable motherhood, you will find an enduring steady stream of unconditional love. Regardless of the situation, an unstoppable mom's love for her children remains constant. This love transcends the clichéd notion of pampering and acquiescing to every whim of your child. Instead, it finds expression in setting limits, enforcing discipline, and occasionally making tough decisions, all underpinned by your child's well-being.

Unconditional love is not about overlooking faults or turning a blind eye to misbehavior. On the contrary, it is about holding children accountable for their actions, setting boundaries, and imparting valuable life lessons. It's about teaching them the consequences of their actions, cultivating a sense of responsibility, and instilling values that will guide them throughout life. The unstoppable mom understands that love, in its truest form, often means saying no, setting limits, and enforcing discipline.

Despite the occasional tears or temporary dissatisfaction, an unstoppable mom stands firm in her decisions, knowing that her choices are rooted in love and concern for her child's future. She comprehends that the immediate gratification derived from conceding to a child's demands cannot compare to the long-term benefits of discipline and structure.

Moreover, unstoppable moms recognize that tough love, when balanced with warmth and affection, helps children feel secure. They ensure that their children understand the motivation behind their decisions and actions. They communicate openly, ensuring their children know that even when they are disciplined, they are still deeply loved. This approach fosters a healthy relationship where children feel secure, understood, and loved, regardless of their actions.

Unconditional love also means accepting and celebrating your children for who they are and fostering an environment where they feel valued and respected. It involves acknowledging their unique strengths, appreciating their individuality, and supporting them in their interests and passions. This unconditional acceptance and affirmation boosts your children's self-esteem and sense of self-worth.

Unstoppable moms understand that unconditional love involves self-sacrifice. At times, it means putting your child's needs ahead of your own, making tough decisions for your child's benefit, and constantly being there for your child, even when it's challenging. This selflessness doesn't mean losing yourself in the process. Unstoppable moms know that self-care does not conflict with unconditional love, but rather, it is a vital part of it.

Unconditional love is the compass guiding unstoppable moms through the complex journey of parenting. It manifests in discipline, setting limits, making tough decisions, accepting and celebrating individuality, and self-sacrifice. This love, consistent and unwavering, lays the foundation for secure, confident children, teaching them the essence of love, not as a mere sentiment, but as a profound commitment to another's well-being. While navigating the labyrinth of motherhood, unstoppable moms anchor themselves in the power of unconditional love, making it their guiding star.

To me, unconditional love means I will always love my children, no matter what they do. But, I will also set boundaries and expectations for them, and hold them accountable. They may not always like the boundaries or the expectations and they certainly may prefer not to be held accountable but these strategies will pay off big time as they grow up and become more independent. My son Nathaniel is the youngest of five children. Some may say I was easier on him than his older siblings and maybe I was. But somewhere in his life, he learned to set his own boundaries, create his own expectations and hold himself accountable. Nathaniel applied for and tested into a rigorous college-prep high school program. With very little prodding from me, he determined what he could and could not do while going to school. He set expectations for himself that were achievable and held himself to a high standard. And he made himself accountable for the heavy work load and study requirements. I like to believe that through our unconditional love, his father and I helped to teach him some of these all-important skills.

As another example of the impact a mom has when she shows unconditional love to her children, let's take a look at a story about a mom named Heidi:

Heidi was a mother of three. She had always been a loving and caring parent. However, as life became busier and more demanding, she sometimes found herself getting frustrated and overwhelmed by the challenges of parenthood. She often felt that her love for her family was conditional on their behavior and achievements, and this mindset was taking a toll on her relationships.

One evening, after a particularly tough day, Heidi sat down to reflect on her parenting journey. She realized that her children and her husband needed her love and support unconditionally, regardless of their actions

MINDSET #4 - UNCONDITIONAL LOVE

or accomplishments. She understood that true love meant being there for her family through thick and thin, without judgment or expectation.

With this realization, Heidi decided to shift her mindset towards showing unconditional love to her family. She began by actively reminding herself of this commitment every day. When her children made mistakes or behaved in challenging ways, instead of reacting with anger or disappointment, she took a deep breath and approached the situation with empathy and understanding.

Heidi also started having open and honest conversations with her family. She encouraged her children to express their feelings and concerns without fear of judgment. She let them know that she loved them no matter what, and that her love was unwavering and constant.

As time passed, Heidi's family began to notice the change in her. They felt a greater sense of security and comfort in their home. Her children became more open with her, sharing their struggles and triumphs without hesitation. Her husband felt more supported and loved, knowing that he had a partner who stood by him through all of life's challenges.

One day, Heidi's oldest child, Sarah, came to her with tears in her eyes after a difficult day at school. Instead of scolding her or trying to fix the problem, Heidi simply hugged her tightly and said, "I love you, Sarah, and I'm here for you no matter what. We'll get through this together." Sarah felt an immense sense of relief and gratitude, realizing that her mother's love was truly unconditional.

Through her mindset shift, Heidi discovered the profound value of showing unconditional love to her family. She learned that this kind of love not only strengthened their bonds but also brought a sense of peace and happiness into their lives. Heidi felt a newfound sense of fulfillment as a mother, knowing that her love was the steady anchor that her family could always rely on.

Heidi's family, in turn, saw her as a source of unwavering support and love. They knew that, no matter what challenges they faced, they had a mother and partner who would stand by them with open arms and a heart full of unconditional love. This change transformed their family dynamic and made their home a place filled with warmth, acceptance, and love.

Unconditional love is a crucial aspect of successful motherhood. The following are examples of how you can demonstrate unconditional love. After each example, you will find three specific actions you can take to model and strengthen your unconditional love mindset. Read through them and choose at least one example that resonates with you. Then, try at least one of the actions and see how it makes you feel. Remember, changing a mindset takes time and the more you practice, the easier it gets.

<u>Being there in times of need</u>: Regardless of the situation, a mom's presence and support in times of need is a strong testament to unconditional love.
- Being Available: Being available means not only making time in your schedule but also prioritizing your child's needs and actively participating in their lives. Whether it's attending school events, helping with homework, or simply being there to listen during a tough day, you show your commitment to being present and supportive in both big and small moments. This consistent presence reassures your child that they can always count on you when they need guidance or a caring presence.
- Provide Comfort and Reassurance: Offer physical and emotional comfort to your child. This may involve hugging them, holding their hand, or simply sitting with them. Reassure them that you are there for them, that you love them unconditionally, and that you will help them through whatever difficulty they are facing.
- Problem-Solving Together: If the situation calls for it, engage in problem-solving together. Encourage your child to brainstorm solutions, and guide them in evaluating their options. Teach them valuable problem-solving and coping skills that they can use in the future. This approach not only addresses the immediate need but also

empowers them to become more resilient.

Expressing Love Verbally and Physically: Saying "I love you" regularly and showing affection through hugs, kisses, or a comforting hand are direct ways a mom shows love.
- Verbal Affirmations: Offer verbal expressions of love regularly. Tell your child "I love you" every day, and use specific affirmations to highlight what you love about them. For example, "I love your creativity" or "I'm so proud of your hard work in school." Compliments and words of encouragement build your child's self-esteem and reinforce your love.
- Physical Affection: Physical touch is a powerful way to convey love. Hug, cuddle, and kiss your child affectionately. Physical affection provides comfort and security and helps your child feel valued and loved. Show physical affection in both ordinary moments and during times when your child may need comfort or reassurance.
- Quality Time Together: Spending quality time with your child is another way to express love. Engage in activities they enjoy, whether it's playing games, reading together, or going for a walk. This dedicated time strengthens your connection and demonstrates your love through actions and presence.

Forgiving Mistakes: Everyone makes mistakes, including children. A mother shows unconditional love by forgiving her child's mistakes and helping them learn and grow from these experiences.
- Acknowledge the Mistake: Start by acknowledging the mistake, either your own or someone else's. It's essential to recognize that mistakes happen and that they are a part of being human. Avoid denial or blame, and instead, accept the reality of the situation.
- Express Forgiveness: Communicate your forgiveness to your child when they make a mistake. Use clear and empathetic language to

convey that you understand the mistake, you don't hold it against them, and you're willing to move forward. For example, say, "I forgive you for what happened, and I'm ready to put it behind us."
- Let Go and Focus on the Future: Once forgiveness is extended, make a conscious effort to let go of any lingering negative feelings or resentment. Refrain from bringing up the mistake repeatedly or holding it against your child. Focus on moving forward and working together to prevent similar mistakes in the future.

Being Patient and Understanding: Love means accepting your child as they are, including their strengths and weaknesses. Showing patience and understanding, especially during challenging times, is a powerful expression of love.
- "Being There" for Your Child: Being present with a calm and understanding presence is a powerful way to demonstrate unconditional love. Stop what you are doing, focus 100% on your child and listen to their thoughts and feelings – good or bad – without getting impatient, angry or frustrated. This shows your child they are important, you care about what they are thinking and you want to hear what they have to say.
- Empathize and Validate Feelings: Put yourself in your child's shoes and try to understand their emotions and point of view. Acknowledge their feelings by saying things like, "I can see why you might feel that way" or "It sounds like you're going through a tough time." Validating someone's feelings shows that you respect and empathize with their experience.
- Give Space and Time: Recognize that your child may need time and space to process their thoughts and emotions. Sometimes, it's beneficial to step back and allow them the freedom to work through their feelings at their own pace. Avoid rushing or pressuring them to come to a resolution or decision.

MINDSET #4 - UNCONDITIONAL LOVE

<u>Encouraging and Supporting</u>: Unconditional love is about believing in your child's abilities, supporting their interests, and cheering them on every step of the way.

- Offer Words of Encouragement: Provide sincere and specific words of encouragement. Let your child know that you believe in their abilities and efforts. For example, say, "You've worked so hard on this project, and I have confidence that you can do it," or "I'm proud of how determined you are to get this done."
- Provide Practical Assistance: Offer your help and assistance when needed. Whether it's offering a hand with a task, providing resources, or lending a listening ear, your practical support can make a significant difference. Actions like, "I'm here to help you with whatever you need," or "Let's tackle this together," show your commitment to their success.
- Celebrate Achievements: Celebrate your child's accomplishments, no matter how small. Recognize and acknowledge their progress and successes along the way. Celebratory gestures like a high five, a note of congratulations, or a heartfelt celebration can boost their confidence and motivation.

<u>Protecting and Providing</u>: Your unconditional love is shown in your constant effort to ensure your child's safety, well being, and provision of their needs—physical, emotional, and psychological.

- Ensuring Safety: Your primary role is to ensure your child's safety and well-being. This includes childproofing your home, monitoring your children's activities, and teaching them about potential dangers. You often set rules and boundaries to keep your children safe from harm.
- Providing Emotional Support: You provide emotional support by being a constant source of love, care, and comfort. You offer a

nurturing and secure environment in which your child can express their feelings, ask questions, and seek guidance. A mom's presence and empathy are invaluable for a child's emotional development.
- Meeting Basic Needs: Moms are responsible for meeting their child's basic needs, including food, clothing, and shelter. You ensure that your child has access to nutritious meals, clean clothes, and a safe and comfortable home. Providing these essentials is fundamental to your child's physical health and development.

<u>Setting Boundaries and Disciplining</u>: Unconditional love also means setting boundaries that help your children understand acceptable behavior. Although disciplining might be tough, it comes from a place of wanting your child to develop good values and behavior.
- Clear Communication of Expectations: Clearly communicate your expectations and rules to your child. Use simple language and provide reasons behind the rules when appropriate. For example, say, "In our house, we don't hit others because it hurts them, and we want everyone to feel safe and happy."
- Consistent Consequences: Establish consequences for breaking rules and consistently apply them. Make sure the consequences are appropriate for the offense and age-appropriate. For instance, if a child doesn't complete their homework, a consequence might be that they can't play with their favorite toy until it's finished. Be consistent in enforcing consequences so that your child understands the connection between their actions and the outcomes.
- Positive Reinforcement and Encouragement: Reinforce positive behavior with praise and encouragement. When your child follows the rules or demonstrates good behavior, acknowledge it with positive feedback. This positive reinforcement helps motivate them to make better choices. For example, say, "I'm so proud of how well you shared your toys with your friend today."

MINDSET #4 - UNCONDITIONAL LOVE

<u>Listening and Empathizing</u>: Taking the time to listen and empathize with a child's feelings, thoughts, and ideas shows a mom's unconditional love.
- Active Listening: When your child is going through a challenging or emotional period, practice active listening. Give them your full attention, maintain eye contact, and avoid interrupting. Allow them to express their feelings and thoughts. Listen without judgment or jumping to conclusions. Show empathy by nodding, validating their feelings, and asking open-ended questions to better understand their perspective. Sometimes, all a child needs is someone to listen and validate their emotions.
- Reflective Responses: Respond to your child's words with empathy and understanding. Reflect back what you've heard to validate their feelings and let them know you're truly listening. For example, say, "It sounds like you had a really tough day at school, and you felt left out during lunch. That must have been hard."
- Offer Emotional Support: Let the person know that you care about their feelings and well-being. Offer comfort, encouragement, and reassurance. Be there for them without judgment or the need to fix their problems. Simply provide a supportive presence.

<u>Making Sacrifices</u>: Whether it's giving up her time, comfort, or personal aspirations, a mom often makes sacrifices for her children, demonstrating her unconditional love.
- Prioritizing Others' Needs: Put the needs and well-being of others before your own when appropriate and necessary. For example, sacrificing your personal time to take care of a sick family member or volunteering to help a friend in need demonstrates your commitment to their welfare.
- Setting Aside Personal Goals: Sometimes, achieving personal goals may require temporarily setting them aside to address more immediate or pressing concerns. This could involve delaying personal projects

or aspirations to focus on family, health, or other essential matters.
- Financial Sacrifices: Financial sacrifices may involve redirecting resources to support the needs of others. This can include contributing financially to family members' education, medical expenses, or emergencies, even if it means adjusting your own spending or saving plans.

<u>Creating a Safe, Loving Environment</u>: Providing a home where your child feels safe, secure, and loved, no matter what, is perhaps one of the most significant ways a mom shows unconditional love.
- Open Communication: Encourage open and honest communication among family members or within your social circles. Create an atmosphere where everyone feels comfortable expressing their thoughts, feelings, and concerns without fear of judgment or criticism. Active listening and empathy play key roles in fostering open communication.
- Affection and Support: Show affection and provide emotional support regularly to your children. Offer physical gestures of love, such as hugs, kisses, and warm embraces. Offer words of affirmation, appreciation, and encouragement to reinforce feelings of love and support. Let your children know that you care deeply for their well-being.
- Respect and Boundaries: Respect personal boundaries and encourage mutual respect among family members or friends. Recognize that everyone has their own space, preferences, and needs. Teach and model respectful behavior, and ensure that everyone's boundaries are honored to create a safe and comfortable environment.

<u>Nurturing Their Individuality</u>: Unconditional love means accepting and celebrating your child's unique personality and talents. This includes

MINDSET #4 - UNCONDITIONAL LOVE

encouraging their individual interests, even if they're different from your own.

- Encourage Self-Expression: Allow your child to express their thoughts, feelings, and interests freely. Encourage them to share their opinions and ideas, even if they differ from your own. Listen attentively and validate their unique perspective, helping them feel heard and valued.
- Support Their Interests and Passions: Identify your child's interests, hobbies, and talents, and support their pursuit of these passions. Enroll them in activities or classes that align with their interests, and provide the necessary resources and encouragement to help them develop their skills and explore their passions.
- Respect Their Choices and Independence: As your child grows, respect their growing sense of independence. Allow them to make age-appropriate choices and decisions, even if they differ from what you might prefer. This fosters a sense of autonomy and personal responsibility.

Standing up for Them: If your child is facing an issue at school or in their social life, standing up for them and being their advocate shows your unconditional love and support.

- Advocate for Their Needs: Be a strong advocate for your child's needs, especially in educational, healthcare, or social settings. If you believe that your child's rights or well-being are not being properly addressed, speak up on their behalf. This may involve communicating with teachers, healthcare providers, or other relevant individuals to ensure your child's needs are met.
- Role Play with Your Child: Modeling to your child through example and role-playing is an excellent way to give your child the confidence to politely and respectfully advocate for his or herself. When your

child is facing a tough conversation with a friend or sibling or needs to advocate for themselves with a teacher or other adult, practicing the conversation with them will give your child the confidence and experience to handle the situation on their own. This is an excellent way to teach your child about self-advocacy so they learn to stand up for themselves when necessary.
- Teach Assertiveness and Boundaries: Empower your child with the skills to assert themselves respectfully and set boundaries. Teach them to communicate their needs and preferences clearly and confidently. Role-play situations with them to help them practice assertive communication.

Apologizing When Necessary: Everyone makes mistakes, including moms. Apologizing when you're wrong shows your child that you respect them and that your love doesn't hinge on always being right.
- Acknowledge the Mistake: Begin by acknowledging the specific mistake or behavior that led to the need for an apology. Clearly state what you did wrong or how your actions may have hurt or upset your child. For example, say, "I'm sorry for yelling at you when I was upset."
- Express Sincere Regret: Express genuine remorse and regret for your actions. Let your child know that you understand the impact of your behavior on them and that you genuinely feel sorry. Use empathetic language like, "I can see how my actions hurt your feelings, and I'm truly sorry for that."
- Commit to Change: Make a commitment to change your behavior in the future. Explain how you plan to avoid making the same mistake and what steps you'll take to improve. For example, you might say, "I will work on managing my frustration better so that I don't yell in the future."

MINDSET #4 - UNCONDITIONAL LOVE

Prioritizing Their Needs: This could be as simple as choosing to spend time playing with your child instead of doing a non-urgent task, or as significant as making career or lifestyle choices that support your child's wellbeing.

- Meeting Basic Needs: Ensure that your child's basic needs are consistently met. This includes providing them with nutritious meals, a safe and comfortable living environment, access to healthcare, and opportunities for physical activity and rest. Meeting these fundamental needs lays a strong foundation for their physical and emotional well-being.
- Balancing Structure and Flexibility: Create a structured routine that balances your child's need for predictability with opportunities for flexibility and choice. A structured environment helps your child feel secure while still allowing for some flexibility and empowering them to make decisions and develop independence.
- Let Your Child Choose: There are many times moms make decisions for their children about what to do, when, and how. When you can, give your child the opportunity to give their opinion or to choose. If you plan to spend a Saturday together, you can ask your child what he or she would like to do. Or, give them a couple of options and ask them to choose. This lets your child know you value their opinion and are prioritizing their needs and desires.

Reassuring Them During Tough Times: Whether they're scared during a thunderstorm or anxious about a test, being there to comfort and reassure them shows your unconditional love.

- Provide Emotional Support: Offer emotional support by being present and available to listen to your child's concerns and feelings. Let them know that it's okay to feel upset or anxious and that you are there to comfort and support them. Give them your full attention and offer comforting words and gestures like hugs.

- Normalize Their Feelings: Help your child understand that their feelings are normal and valid. Share examples from your own experiences to show that everyone faces challenges and difficult emotions at times. Normalize the idea that it's okay to seek help or talk to someone they trust when they need support.
- Problem-Solve Together: Encourage problem-solving by working together to find solutions to the challenges they are facing. Empower your child to brainstorm ideas and make decisions, even if they're small. Involving them in the problem-solving process can boost their confidence and resilience.

<u>Respecting Their Feelings</u>: Allowing your child to experience their feelings, even negative ones, and supporting them through those feelings can be a powerful demonstration of love.

- Stop and Listen: Take the time to focus on your child and give them the opportunity to express their feelings or concerns. Give them your full attention. Show empathy by nodding, paraphrasing their words, and using phrases like, "I understand how you feel," or "Tell me more about what's bothering you." (Giving your child your full attention and listening is such an important action – you will notice it is mentioned many times throughout this book!)
- Validate Their Emotions: Acknowledge and validate your child's emotions, even if you don't necessarily agree with their perspective. Let them know that it's okay to feel the way they do. For example, say, "It's okay to be angry about this," or "I can see why you're feeling sad right now."
- Respect Their Privacy: Respect your child's need for privacy and personal space, especially as they grow older. Avoid prying into their emotions or demanding that they share their feelings if they're not comfortable doing so. Give them the autonomy to express themselves when they're ready.

Consistently Being There: Regularly showing up for all the little things, like family dinners, bedtime stories, or just asking about their day, can show a child that they're loved no matter what.
- Regular Quality Time: Dedicate regular quality time to spend with your child. Engage in activities they enjoy, such as playing games, reading together, or going for walks. Consistently setting aside time for bonding helps create a sense of security and connection.
- Consistent Routine: Establish a consistent daily routine that includes predictable mealtimes, bedtime, and other essential activities. Consistency provides structure and stability in your child's life, making them feel safe and secure.
- Active Participation: Be actively involved in your child's life by showing interest in their activities, schoolwork, and hobbies. Attend their school events, extracurricular activities, and parent-teacher conferences. Show your support by being present during important moments in their life.

Teaching Them: Spending the time to teach your child various skills, from tying their shoelaces to complex life skills, shows your unconditional love and desire for them to succeed.
- Model Behavior: Lead by example and model the behaviors and values you want to instill in your child. Whether it's kindness, respect, responsibility, or any other important trait, your actions and interactions serve as powerful teaching tools.
- Encourage Exploration and Curiosity: Foster a love for learning by encouraging your child to explore their interests and ask questions. Provide opportunities for hands-on learning and discovery through activities like experiments, visits to museums, or nature walks.
- Provide Guidance and Feedback: Offer guidance and constructive feedback when teaching your child new skills or concepts. Be patient

and supportive, allowing them to make mistakes and learn from them. Encourage their efforts and celebrate their achievements, no matter how small.

Allowing Them To Make Mistakes: This can be hard for moms, but allowing your child to make their own mistakes and be there to support them afterward is an important part of unconditional love.
- Provide a Safe Environment: Create a safe and supportive environment where your child feels comfortable taking risks and making mistakes. Let them know that it's okay to make errors and that they won't face harsh consequences for trying new things or experimenting.
- Offer Guidance, Not Control: Instead of micromanaging your child's actions, provide guidance and support. Encourage them to think critically and problem-solve on their own. Offer suggestions and share your own experiences when appropriate, but allow them the freedom to make decisions and learn from the outcomes.
- Discuss and Reflect: After a mistake has been made, engage in open and non-judgmental discussions with your child. Ask questions like, "What did you learn from this experience?" or "What would you do differently next time?" Encourage them to reflect on their actions and draw valuable lessons from their mistakes.

Respecting Their Autonomy: As your child grows older, respecting their choices and their autonomy – even when you disagree – shows that your love for them is not dependent on them making the choices you would prefer.
- Offer Choices: Allow your child to make age-appropriate choices in various aspects of their life, such as clothing, food, or leisure activities. Provide options whenever possible, so they have the opportunity to express their preferences and make decisions.

- Encourage Independence: Support your child in developing independence by allowing them to take on age-appropriate responsibilities and tasks. Encourage them to solve problems on their own, make choices, and learn from their experiences. Offer guidance when needed, but avoid over controlling their actions.
- Support Their Passions: Supporting your child's passions involves taking an active interest in their pursuits, whether it's attending their soccer games, helping them with a science project, or simply showing enthusiasm for their artistic creations. This not only fosters a sense of autonomy but also strengthens the parent-child bond by demonstrating that you value your child's unique interests and talents, even when they may not align with your own preferences.

***

While unconditional love is crucial, it does not mean indulging every whim or desire of your child. It's about valuing your child for who they are, not what they do, and providing a supportive, caring environment for them to grow and flourish. Unconditional love is about a consistent pattern of love and respect, regardless of disagreements, challenges, or your child's behavior at any given moment.

Chapter Summary

• **Unconditional Love is the Foundation:** Unconditional love is central to being an unstoppable mom. It involves loving your child at all times while setting limits, enforcing discipline, and making tough decisions, all rooted in your child's well-being.

• **Hold Your Children Accountable and Set Boundaries:** Unconditional love doesn't mean ignoring faults or misbehaviors. It's about holding children accountable, setting boundaries, and imparting life lessons, teaching them responsibility and instilling values.

• **Discipline Rooted in Love:** An unstoppable mom understands that love often means saying no and enforcing discipline, focusing on long-term benefits over immediate gratification.

• **Balancing Tough Love with Warmth:** Tough love, when balanced with warmth and affection, helps children feel secure. Ensure your children understand the motivations behind your decisions, reinforcing that discipline doesn't diminish love.

• **Celebrate Individuality:** Unconditional love involves accepting and celebrating your child for who they are, fostering an environment where they feel valued and respected. This boosts self-esteem and sense of self-worth.

• **Self-Sacrifice and Self-Care:** Unconditional love often involves self-sacrifice and prioritizing your child's needs, yet unstoppable moms recognize that self-care is also an integral part of unconditional love.

• **The Guiding Compass of Parenting:** Unconditional love guides unstoppable moms through the complexities of parenting. It manifests in various ways including discipline, setting limits, acceptance, and self-sacrifice, all laying a foundation for secure and confident children.

Chapter 10

Mindset #5 - Mindful Presence

The Heartbeat of Connection in an Unstoppable Mom

> *"A mother understands what a child does not say."*
> - Jewish Proverb

In the symphony of unstoppable motherhood, one note rings clear and consistent above all others: the note of mindful presence. An unstoppable mom aims to be present - truly present - and in the moment. While the never-ending call of responsibilities and distractions might be loud, unstoppable moms strive to tune themselves into a different rhythm - the rhythm of being fully present when you are with your children, cherishing your shared time as the sacred time it is.

In an era defined by constant connectivity and endless multitasking, maintaining a mindful presence can be a daunting challenge. Yet, the essence of mindful presence lies in its simplicity: It means being fully engaged in the current moment, immersing yourself in the now. When you are with your children, you are not just physically there but also emotionally and mentally present. You listen attentively, respond thoughtfully, and observe keenly.

My son Joshua was the best when it came to reminding me of the importance of being mindfully present when interacting with my children.

MINDSET #5 - MINDFUL PRESENCE

When Joshua wanted attention, he would get as close to me as possible. His favorite place was sitting on my lap. Once he was comfortable, he would begin to talk and if he didn't think I was fully focused on him, he would put his little hand on my chin and turn my face towards his. He never missed a word in his conversation and his expression never changed as he moved my face so I could look right at him. This was a gentle reminder to me of the importance of giving my children my undivided attention and looking them in the eyes when we were talking to each other.

This mindful presence carries profound implications. It communicates to your children that they are valued and that their thoughts, feelings, and experiences matter. When a child feels seen and heard, it bolsters their confidence, fosters secure attachment and a sense of caring, enhances their emotional well-being, and strengthens their resilience.

Mindful presence lets an unstoppable mom truly connect with her children. It's in these moments of shared presence that memories are created, bonds are strengthened, and love is deeply felt. It could be as simple as sharing laughter over a joke, engaging in a heartfelt conversation, or jointly marveling at the beauty of a sunset. These moments of connection, though seemingly small, form the cherished pieces of a child's memory.

Being mindfully present also means you are tuned into your own thoughts and feelings. You understand that your emotional state can influence your interactions with your children. So, you cultivate self-awareness, build patience, strive to manage your emotions and model emotional resilience. Your mindful presence benefits not just your children but also yourself.

In the dynamic dance of motherhood, being mindfully present also helps you navigate the changes going on around you. You are more likely to notice the subtle shifts in your child's behavior, catch the early signs of any problems, and promptly address any concerns.

Mindful presence is the heartbeat of connection in unstoppable motherhood. It communicates love, fosters connection, and enhances understanding. While being mindfully present amidst your many responsibilities can be challenging, the rewards are profound. As you navigate the symphony of motherhood, you value and nurture mindful presence, allowing it to be the consistent, resonating note that harmonizes your relationship with your children.

As an example of the impact a mom has when she keeps a mindful presence, lets take a look at a story about a mom named Terri:

Terri was a mother of three young children, and like many parents, she often found herself overwhelmed by the demands of motherhood and the constant busyness of life. She was always multitasking; juggling work, household chores, and her children's activities. Her mind was often racing, and she rarely had a moment to pause and simply be present with her family.

One day, as Terri was rushing through her morning routine, she happened to overhear a conversation between her children, Emma, Jamie and Max. They were talking about how they wished they could spend more focused time with her and how they missed just being together as a family.

Terri's heart sank as she realized how her busy and distracted lifestyle was affecting her children. She knew that something needed to change. She had heard about the concept of mindfulness and decided to explore it as a way to bring more presence and balance into her life.

Terri began her mindfulness journey by setting aside a few minutes each day to practice meditation. She found a quiet corner in her home where she could sit in peace, close her eyes, and focus on her breath. At first, her mind wandered constantly, but she didn't get discouraged. She reminded herself that mindfulness was a skill that required practice.

MINDSET #5 - MINDFUL PRESENCE

As the days turned into weeks, Terri noticed a subtle but powerful shift within herself. She started to become more aware of her thoughts and emotions as they arose. She realized that being present meant fully engaging with whatever she was doing, whether it was playing with her children, cooking a meal, or simply listening to her children and husband talk about their day.

Terri made an effort to put away her phone and other distractions when she was with her family. She learned to savor the moments, finding joy in the simple things like watching her children play, listening to their laughter, and engaging in meaningful conversations.

As a result of her mindful presence, Terri's relationship with her children blossomed. They felt heard, valued, and cherished. Terri no longer rushed through their interactions but took the time to connect on a deeper level. She noticed her children's smiles, their quirks, and their unique personalities in ways she hadn't before.

Her husband also benefited from this transformation. With her newfound presence and focus on mindfulness, their relationship grew stronger as they communicated more openly and connected on a deeper emotional level.

Terri's journey into a mindful presence mindset had a profound impact on her life. She found that she was happier, more patient, and less stressed. She learned that the true value of being present was not just about creating lasting memories with her family but also about finding peace and contentment within herself.

Her children saw the change in their mother and felt the love and attention she now gave them. They cherished the moments they spent together and felt the warmth of her presence. Terri had learned that being mindful and fully present in the moment was one of the greatest gifts she could give to her family and to herself.

The beauty of mindful presence is that it can be cultivated in any situation. The following are examples of how you can demonstrate mindful presence. After each example, you will find three specific actions you can take to model and strengthen your mindful presence. Read through them and choose at least one example that resonates with you. Then, try at least one of the actions and see how it makes you feel. Remember, changing a mindset takes time and the more you practice, the easier it gets.

<u>During Meal Times</u>: Instead of rushing through meals or multitasking, you take the time to sit and eat with your children. You're fully present, enjoying the taste of your food and the company of your family. You listen attentively to your children's stories and engage in meaningful conversation.

- Engage in Mindful Eating: Encourage everyone at the table, including yourself, to eat mindfully. This means savoring each bite, paying attention to the flavors and textures of the food, and eating slowly. Avoid distractions like phones or TV, and instead, focus on the meal and the company.
- Converse and Connect: Use meal times as an opportunity for meaningful conversation. Ask open-ended questions about your child's day, interests, or thoughts. Listen actively to their responses and engage in the discussion. Share your own stories and experiences, creating a sense of connection and bonding.
- Express Gratitude: Begin or end the meal with a moment of gratitude. Encourage each family member to express something they are thankful for that day. This practice fosters a positive and appreciative atmosphere, reinforcing the value of togetherness and shared meals.

<u>When Your Child is Speaking to You</u>: You listen with your full attention, making eye contact, and responding in a way that shows you're engaged.

You're not distracted by your phone, TV, or other tasks. Even if you're busy, you take a moment to give your child your undivided attention.

- Eye Contact and Active Listening: When your child starts to speak, make a conscious effort to maintain eye contact with them. Put down any distractions, such as your phone or a book, and show that you are fully engaged in the conversation. Listen actively by nodding, using encouraging verbal cues like "I see" or "Tell me more," and avoiding interruptions.
- Empathetic Responses: Respond to your child's words with empathy and understanding. Acknowledge their feelings and experiences by saying things like, "I can see that you're feeling really excited about that," or "It sounds like you had a tough day." This validates their emotions and encourages them to open up further.
- Ask Open-Ended Questions: Encourage your child to share more by asking open-ended questions that invite deeper discussion. For example, instead of asking, "Did you have a good day at school?" you can ask, "What was the most interesting thing that happened at school today?" This helps them express themselves more fully and promotes meaningful conversation.

During Playtime: You actively engage in play with your child, following their lead. You're not thinking about your to-do list or checking your phone. You're present in the moment, sharing laughter and joy with your child.

- Engage Actively and Fully: During playtime with your child, you can cultivate a mindful presence by fully immersing yourself in the moment. First and foremost, put away distractions like your phone or other devices, ensuring your complete focus on your child and the play activity. Engage actively in the play, whether it's building with blocks, playing a board game, or creating art. By participating

with enthusiasm and curiosity, you not only show your child that you value their play but also deepen your connection.
- Practice Non-Judgmental Observation: During playtime, practice non-judgmental observation. Allow your child to take the lead in the play, and follow their cues and imagination. Instead of directing or critiquing, simply observe their actions and listen to their narratives without judgment. This promotes a sense of autonomy and creativity in your child's play, fostering their self-expression and problem-solving skills.
- Embrace the Joy of Play: During playtime with your child, embrace the joy of the experience without worrying about the outcome or productivity. Let go of any agenda or rush to finish a task. Instead, savor the present moment, relishing in the laughter, curiosity, and shared experiences. Mindful playtime creates a space for you and your child to bond, explore, and create memories together, strengthening your relationship and fostering a sense of wonder.

<u>When Helping With Homework</u>: You give your full attention to helping your child understand their assignments. You're patient, guiding them through difficult problems rather than rushing to provide answers.
- Create a Distraction-Free Environment: When it's time for homework, set up a quiet and organized workspace where your child can focus without distractions. Turn off the TV, limit noise, and keep electronic devices away unless they're necessary for the assignment. By creating a calm and focused environment, you help your child concentrate and be present in the task at hand.
- Offer Guidance with Patience and Empathy: When your child encounters challenges or struggles with a particular concept, approach their difficulties with patience and empathy. Instead of rushing to provide answers, ask open-ended questions that guide

them to think critically and problem-solve. Show understanding of their frustrations and reassure them that it's okay to make mistakes. By being empathetic and supportive, you create a safe space for your child to learn and grow.
- Practice Active Listening and Feedback: Engage in active listening while your child explains their homework or discusses their thoughts and questions. Give them your full attention, maintain eye contact, and nod to show you're actively involved in the conversation. Offer constructive feedback and praise their efforts rather than just focusing on correctness. By actively participating in the learning process and acknowledging their progress, you reinforce their confidence and motivation to excel.

<u>During Bedtime Rituals</u>: You maintain a calm and relaxed atmosphere during bedtime. Whether you're getting things ready for the next day, reading a story, or simply tucking your child in, you're fully present, making this a special and comforting time for your child.
- Establish a Calm and Consistent Routine: Begin by creating a calming bedtime routine that unfolds at the same time each night. This routine might include activities like packing up backpacks, picking out clothes for the next day, making lunches, reading a bedtime story, taking a warm bath, or practicing deep breathing exercises together. By following a consistent routine, you help your child anticipate and ease into bedtime, promoting a sense of security and tranquility.
- Be Fully Present During Bedtime Activities: During each element of the bedtime routine, be fully present and engaged with your child. Whether you're getting ready for the next day, reading a book, or brushing teeth, give your child your undivided attention. Put away distractions like phones or other devices to ensure a tranquil and mindful bedtime experience.

- Encourage Reflective Conversations: Use bedtime as an opportunity for reflective conversations with your child. Ask them about their day, their thoughts, and their feelings. Listen actively and empathetically to what they share. Create a space where your child feels comfortable expressing themselves and discussing any concerns they may have. By fostering open and nurturing conversations, you provide your child with emotional support and a sense of connection before they drift off to sleep.

When You Notice Your Child's Emotions: You're attuned to your child's feelings and respond with empathy. You validate their emotions, whether they're happy, sad, or angry, and provide comfort when needed.

- Validate Their Feelings: "I see you're feeling [emotion]. It's okay to feel that way." This acknowledgment reassures your child that their emotions are valid and understood. It creates a safe space for them to express themselves without judgment, fostering trust and emotional connection.
- Offer a Listening Ear: Ask your child, "Do you want to talk about it? I'm here to listen." By offering to listen, you're showing that you care about their thoughts and feelings. This act demonstrates genuine concern and can make your child feel valued and less isolated in their emotions.
- Physical Comfort: Offer a hug or comforting touch, saying, "I'm here for you if you need a hug." Physical gestures like hugs release oxytocin, a hormone associated with bonding and comfort. This touch can provide immediate relief from distress, reinforcing a sense of security and emotional support.

When Spending Time in Nature: Whether you're going for a walk in the park, or having a picnic, you appreciate the beauty of the surroundings with your child. You help them observe and connect with nature, instead of hurrying through the activity.

- Observe Nature: Take a moment to simply observe and appreciate your natural surroundings. Pay attention to the sounds, smells, and sights of the environment. This practice helps your child develop keen observational and mindfulness skills. By observing nature, they learn patience, focus, and an appreciation for the environment, which can lead to enhanced cognitive development and a broader understanding of the world around them.
- Engage the Senses: Encourage your child to touch leaves, smell flowers, or listen to the birds. Engaging their senses helps them connect more deeply with the natural world.
- Disconnect: Turn off electronic devices or put them on silent to minimize distractions and fully immerse yourself in nature. Disconnecting from electronics allows your child to be present in the moment and reduce potential sensory overload. This promotes better attention span, encourages real-world exploration, and provides a break from screen time, supporting overall mental and physical health.

<u>When Teaching New Skills</u>: You're patient and understanding, focusing on the learning process rather than the result. Whether it's tying shoelaces, baking cookies, or learning to ride a bike, you're there, guiding and supporting them.

- Break It Down: Divide the skill into smaller, manageable steps. Segmenting tasks makes them more digestible and less intimidating for your child. This approach enhances their self-efficacy, helping them feel capable and motivated as they tackle and master each individual step.
- Demonstrate: Show how to perform each step clearly and patiently. Visual demonstrations give your child a concrete example to follow, minimizing confusion. Seeing the skill in action helps solidify their understanding and builds their confidence, as they know exactly

what is expected of them.
- Practice Together: Engage in hands-on practice, providing guidance and support as needed. Collaborative practice fosters a sense of security and support. As your child attempts the skill, they benefit from immediate feedback and assistance, reducing potential frustrations and reinforcing correct techniques. This shared experience also strengthens your bond and encourages open communication about their learning process.

During Moments of Stress: Even when things are chaotic, you maintain your composure and stay present. Instead of letting stress overwhelm you, you take deep breaths, model calm behavior, and tackle one thing at a time.
- Validate Their Feelings: Acknowledge your child's stress by saying, "I can see that you're feeling stressed right now, and that's okay." Let them know it's normal to feel this way sometimes.
- Provide Comfort: Offer physical comfort through a hug or soothing touch. Reassure them that you're there for them and that they can talk to you about what's bothering them.
- Problem-Solve Together: Encourage your child to share what's causing their stress. Help them brainstorm potential solutions or coping strategies. This collaborative problem-solving approach empowers them to manage stress constructively.

When Enjoying Quiet Moments: Whether it's cuddling on the couch, watching the sunset, or simply sitting quietly together, you cherish these moments of peace and connection with your child.
- Silent Presence: Sit or lie down together in silence, simply enjoying each other's company without the need for words. This quiet time allows your child to feel truly seen and valued without the pressure

of conversation or performance. It fosters a deep sense of security, connection, and emotional bonding, letting them know they are loved and cherished just for being themselves.

- Mindful Breathing: Practice mindful breathing together. Inhale deeply and exhale slowly, encouraging your child to focus on their breath. Mindful breathing offers a grounding technique that can help your child manage stress, anxiety, or overwhelming emotions. By practicing together, they not only learn a valuable life skill but also associate it with the comfort and safety of your presence.
- Shared Activity: Engage in a quiet and enjoyable activity, such as reading a book together, drawing, or stargazing. Let the activity unfold naturally without rushing, savoring the tranquility of the moment. Sharing peaceful activities strengthens your bond, enhances your child's appreciation for calm moments, and encourages mindfulness. It provides an opportunity for them to develop patience, focus, and a sense of wonder, while also enjoying quality time with a loved one.

<u>During Morning Routines</u>: When helping your child get ready for the day, you are completely present. Whether it's brushing teeth, dressing, or having breakfast, you're focused on the task and your child, rather than mentally running through your to-do list for the day.

- Establish a Predictable Routine: Create a morning routine with a consistent schedule, so your child knows what to expect. This predictability reduces stress and promotes a sense of security.
- Morning Connection: Spend a few moments connecting with your child. This can be through morning music, a good morning hug, a cheerful greeting, or a short conversation about their plans for the day. It sets a positive tone for the day ahead.
- Mindful Preparation: As you help your child get ready for the day, be present and patient. Assist them with tasks like waking up with a

smile, getting dressed, and preparing breakfast while engaging with them in a calm and unhurried manner. This approach sets a positive tone for the day, reducing morning stress and promoting emotional stability. By being present and attentive, your child feels valued and heard, building their self-esteem. It also teaches them the importance of starting the day with intention and calmness, a lesson they can carry into their own routines as they grow.

<u>When Your Child is Upset</u>: You offer your full attention and presence when your child is feeling down or facing a difficult situation. You offer comfort, validation, and guidance without rushing to "fix" the situation or dismiss their feelings.

- Offer Comfort: Provide physical comfort through a hug or holding their hand. Offer soothing words like, "I'm here for you" or "It's okay to feel this way." This immediate response of comfort and assurance provides your child with a strong sense of security and belonging. It reinforces the idea that they are not alone in their feelings and that they have a safe space with you. Such gestures can significantly reduce anxiety and build your child's emotional resilience.
- Problem-Solve Together: If appropriate, help your child problem-solve the issue that's causing their upset feelings. Encourage them to brainstorm solutions and offer guidance as needed. Engaging in problem-solving together not only addresses the immediate concern but also equips your child with critical thinking skills. It empowers them to handle future challenges proactively and instills a sense of capability and independence. Additionally, the collaborative approach reinforces the idea that they can seek help when needed, nurturing a strong support system for them.
- Stay Calm and Patient: Maintain a calm and patient demeanor, even if your child's emotions are intense. Your own emotional stability can

help them feel more secure and supported during difficult moments.

<u>While Reading Together</u>: You engage fully in the story, making it an interactive and shared experience. You discuss the characters, ask your child questions about the story, and listen attentively to their thoughts and responses.
- Interactive Reading: Encourage your child to actively participate in the story by asking questions like, "What do you think will happen next?" or "Can you find the cat on this page?" This interactive approach invites them to think critically, make predictions, and interact with the book's content.
- Voice Characterization: Use different voices and tones when reading dialogue or narrating various characters. This adds depth and excitement to the storytelling, making the characters come to life and keeping your child engaged in the narrative.
- Discuss and Relate: After reading a portion of the story or finishing the book, take a moment to discuss it with your child. Ask questions like, "What did you like most about the story?" or "Did anything in the book remind you of your own experiences?" This post-reading conversation deepens their comprehension and encourages reflection.

<u>During Bath Time</u>: Rather than rushing through this daily routine, you make it a time of relaxation and bonding. You talk with your child, play with bath toys together, and enjoy the moment.
- Prepare the Bath: Before beginning, double-check that the bathwater temperature is comfortable and safe for your child. Ensure that all bath toys and essential supplies, such as soap and shampoo, are within easy reach to prevent accidents. Constantly supervise your child during the bath to ensure their safety.
- Engage in Play and Learning: Bath time offers a unique opportunity

for play and learning. Provide a variety of bath toys that are safe for water play, such as rubber ducks or floating alphabet letters. Integrating play with learning during bath time not only makes the experience enjoyable but also stimulates cognitive development.

- Encourage Exploration: Encourage your child to explore, splash, and learn about concepts like sinking and floating while having fun. As they engage with toys and explore water properties, they naturally grasp scientific concepts and hone their motor skills.

Nurture Bonding: Use bath time as a bonding experience by engaging in gentle conversation. Talk about your child's day, ask open-ended questions, or simply share stories. Maintain eye contact, smile, and create a warm, nurturing atmosphere. This helps your child feel connected and secure.

- Quality Time Together: Dedicate quality one-on-one time to spend with your child. Engage in activities they enjoy, such as playing games, reading, or exploring the outdoors. During this time, be fully present, actively participate, and focus on creating positive shared experiences.
- Open Communication: Encourage open and honest communication with your child. Create a safe space where they feel comfortable expressing their thoughts, feelings, and concerns. Listen actively, without judgment, and validate their emotions. Respond empathetically and offer guidance when needed.
- Physical Affection: Physical touch is a powerful way to nurture bonding. Offer hugs, cuddles, and physical affection regularly. These gestures convey love, comfort, and security, reinforcing the emotional connection between you and your child.

MINDSET #5 - MINDFUL PRESENCE

<u>When Observing Your Child's Interests</u>: You take the time to really understand what your child is passionate about. Whether it's a favorite book, a hobby, or a sport, you show genuine interest and support.

- Be Attentive: Pay close attention to what activities and subjects captivate your child's attention. Notice when they become engrossed in something, whether it's building with blocks, exploring nature, or reading books. Take mental or written notes to track their interests over time. Being attentive to your child's interests reinforces their sense of self-worth and validates their passions. It sends a clear message that their choices and preferences are valuable. This boosts their self-esteem and encourages them to further pursue and delve into what intrigues them, fostering a love for lifelong learning.
- Provide Resources: Support your child's interests by offering resources, materials, or opportunities related to their passions. This could include books, educational toys, art supplies, or visits to places like museums or nature centers that align with their interests. Providing tailored resources enhances their exploration and deepens their understanding of subjects they're passionate about. This not only nurtures their cognitive growth but also fosters creativity, critical thinking, and a strong sense of autonomy. They feel empowered to dive deeper into their interests, leading to a more enriched and holistic learning experience.
- Engage and Explore Together: Once you've identified your child's interests, actively participate with them. Join in their activities, ask questions, and show genuine curiosity. This not only strengthens your connection but also encourages their exploration and learning.

<u>During Family Outings</u>: On trips to the zoo, park, or even the grocery store, you stay fully engaged with your child. You talk about what you see, ask your child their thoughts and opinions, and make the outing a shared experience.

- Engage in Shared Activities: Plan activities that the whole family can enjoy together, whether it's a hike in the woods, a visit to a zoo, or a day at the beach. Participate actively and encourage your child's involvement, creating a sense of togetherness and shared experiences.
- Include Your Child's Interests: Take into account your child's interests when planning outings. If they have a particular fascination with animals, for instance, choose destinations like a wildlife sanctuary or a petting zoo. Involving their interests ensures they feel valued and excited about the outing.
- Disconnect from Devices: Make a conscious effort to disconnect from electronic devices during family outings. Encourage everyone to be present in the moment, fully engaging with each other and the surroundings. This not only enhances the experience but also sets a positive example for your child about the value of real-life connections.

<u>When Celebrating Achievements</u>: Whether it's a good grade, a sports achievement, or a simple act of kindness, you take the time to acknowledge and celebrate your child's accomplishments. You express your pride and joy in a genuine and present way.

- Express Genuine Pride: Show your genuine pride and excitement for your child's accomplishments. Offer specific praise by acknowledging what they did well. For example, say, "I'm so proud of how hard you worked on your project. Your effort really paid off!" Letting them know you are proud of their work helps them to develop a sense of pride in what they do and accomplish.
- Celebrate Together: Make celebrations a family affair. Plan a special meal, outing, or activity that your child enjoys to mark their achievement. This not only recognizes their success but also reinforces the importance of celebrating milestones together as a family.
- Encourage Goal Setting: After celebrating one achievement,

encourage your child to set new goals. Discuss what they want to achieve next and how they can work toward those goals. This fosters a sense of ambition and a growth mindset.

While Teaching Life Skills: When you're teaching your child how to cook a simple meal, clean up their room, or manage their time, you're fully involved in the process. You provide patient guidance and support, focusing on the teaching moment rather than the end goal.

- Hands-On Learning: Encourage your child to actively participate in learning life skills. Whether it's cooking, doing laundry, or budgeting, involve them in the process. Provide step-by-step guidance and gradually allow them to take on more responsibility as they become proficient. Hands-on learning fosters a deeper understanding and retention of skills compared to passive learning. By actively engaging in tasks, your child gains practical experience, which enhances their confidence and competence. This method of learning also instills a sense of accomplishment and self-reliance, preparing them for future independence.
- Patience and Practice: Understand that acquiring life skills takes time and practice. Be patient and supportive, allowing your child to make mistakes and learn from them. Offer constructive feedback and praise their efforts along the way. Adopting an approach of patience and practice nurtures a growth mindset in your child. They learn that it's okay to make mistakes and that these are opportunities for growth rather than failures. This mindset promotes resilience, adaptability, and a positive attitude towards challenges. By receiving feedback and encouragement, they're motivated to persevere and continually improve, leading to mastery over time.
- Real-Life Application: Look for opportunities to apply life skills in real-life situations. For example, involve your child in meal planning

and grocery shopping to reinforce budgeting and nutrition skills. These practical experiences help them see the relevance of what they're learning.

During Health Check-ups: Doctor's appointments can be stressful for children. Being fully present and attentive during these visits can reassure your child and help them understand the importance of health care.
- Prepare and Explain: Before the appointment, explain to your child what to expect during the check-up. Use age-appropriate language to describe the procedures, such as taking measurements, listening to their heartbeat, or receiving vaccinations. Address any questions or concerns they may have. Preparation and understanding reduce fear of the unknown. When a child knows what to expect, they can mentally prepare, resulting in reduced anxiety and apprehension. This proactive approach fosters trust and confidence, ensuring that medical visits become a normalized and less intimidating experience for them.
- Be Supportive: During the check-up, be a source of comfort and support for your child. Hold their hand, offer reassuring words, and praise their bravery. Stay calm and composed to help alleviate any anxiety they may feel. Your presence and support provide a safety net for your child. They derive strength and assurance from you, helping them navigate potentially stressful situations with greater ease. This reinforces the bond of trust between you and your child, ensuring they feel loved and protected.
- Ask Questions: Don't hesitate to ask questions or seek clarification from the healthcare provider. Discuss any health concerns or changes in your child's behavior or development. Being proactive in seeking information and addressing concerns ensures your child

receives the best possible care. By actively inquiring and addressing concerns, you advocate for your child's well-being. They benefit from thorough care, early intervention (if required), and overall better health outcomes. Additionally, it demonstrates to your child the importance of open communication and proactive care, setting a positive example for their future health habits.

<u>When Acknowledging Mistakes</u>: If your child makes a mistake or misbehaves, you address the issue in a calm and present manner. You focus on the behavior, not the child, and use the situation as a learning opportunity.

- Stay Calm and Patient: Approach the situation with a calm and patient demeanor. Avoid reacting with anger or frustration, as this may discourage your child from being open about their mistakes in the future. Instead, create a safe space for them to discuss what happened.
- Encourage Self-Reflection: Ask open-ended questions that encourage your child to reflect on their actions and the consequences of their mistake. For example, you might say, "Can you tell me what happened?" or "How do you think we can prevent this from happening again?" This promotes critical thinking and problem-solving.
- Teach Responsibility and Accountability: Help your child take responsibility for their mistake and its consequences. Encourage them to make amends if necessary, whether through an apology or by helping to rectify the situation. Emphasize that making mistakes is a natural part of learning and growing.

***

Mindful presence is about quality, not quantity. Even if you have a busy schedule, dedicating small moments of undivided attention to your child can make a significant positive impact. By practicing mindful presence, you not only strengthen your connection with your child but you also model a valuable skill. Mindfulness can help your child navigate their emotions, reduce stress, and enjoy life's simple pleasures.

Chapter Summary

• **Mindful Presence Above All:** In the symphony of unstoppable motherhood, being mindfully present with your children is paramount. Amidst life's distractions, prioritize being fully present, cherishing the time spent with your children as sacred.

• **Embrace the Simplicity of the Moment:** Mindful presence is about fully engaging in the current moment with your children, being there not just physically but also emotionally and mentally.

• **Communicate How Much Your Value Your Children:** By being mindfully present, you communicate to your children that they are valued and important. This attention bolsters their confidence, fosters secure attachment, and strengthens their emotional well-being.

• **Create Memories and Strengthen Bonds:** Shared moments of presence are invaluable in creating lasting memories, strengthening bonds, and deepening your mutual love and understanding.

• **Self-Awareness and Emotional Management:** Being mindfully present also involves being aware of your own emotions and how they influence interactions with your children. Cultivate self-awareness and emotional resilience for beneficial interactions.

• **Navigate the Nuances of Being a Mom:** Mindful presence aids in noticing subtle changes in your child's behavior, allowing you to address concerns promptly and navigate motherhood's dynamic landscape more effectively.

- **Mindful Presence is Important:** Value and nurture mindful presence in your motherhood journey. Mindful presence – being focused and present – strengthens the consistent note that harmonizes your relationship with your children, enhancing love and connection.

- **Cultivate Mindful Presence in Any Situation:** Mindful presence is about quality, not quantity. Even brief moments of undivided attention can significantly impact your child's well-being and your mutual relationship.

Chapter 11

Mindset #6 -
Role Modeling
The Living Lessons Taught by an Unstoppable Mom

> *"The art of mothering is to teach the art of living to children."*
> - Elaine Heffner

In the intricate world of unstoppable motherhood, one aspect towers above all and carries enormous influence: being a role model. As an unstoppable mom, you are cognizant of the impact of your actions, understanding that actions often speak louder than words. You strive to be a living embodiment of the values you wish to instill in your children - kindness, honesty, perseverance, respect, and more. You know you are your children's first and most enduring role model, and you shoulder this responsibility with intention and integrity.

Role modeling is the silent language of parenting. It's an ongoing dialogue conveyed not through words but through actions, attitudes, and behaviors. As such, an unstoppable mom recognizes that every day brings countless opportunities to model values and life skills. You embody kindness in your interactions, display honesty in your dealings, exhibit perseverance in the face of difficulties, and show respect towards everyone.

MINDSET #6 - ROLE MODELING

Beyond exhibiting desirable traits, an unstoppable mom also models how to handle challenges and mistakes. You understand that your children are watching how you react to life's ups and downs. Therefore, you exhibit resilience in the face of setbacks, show patience when things don't go as planned, and handle mistakes with grace and accountability. Through your behavior, you teach your children that it's okay to make mistakes, that challenges can be overcome, and that every situation holds potential for learning and growth.

As an unstoppable mom, you also model healthy habits and self-care. You understand that children learn best from what they observe. So, you take care of your physical health, manage your stress, maintain a balanced lifestyle, and engage in activities you enjoy. Through this, you demonstrate the importance of personal well-being, setting a foundation for your children's lifelong health habits.

Moreover, in being a role model, as an unstoppable mom you respect your children's individuality. You do not seek to mold them into mini versions of yourself but rather encourage them to become the best version of themselves. You celebrate their unique traits and interests and support them in their journeys.

However, being an unstoppable mom is not about being perfect. Instead, you are authentic. You admit your faults, apologize when you're wrong, and share your struggles. By doing so, you model authenticity, humility, and the human side of adulthood.

Role modeling is the living lesson in unstoppable motherhood. It's a silent, powerful language through which a mom shapes her children's values, attitudes, skills, and habits. As an unstoppable mom, you navigate your role as a living lesson with intentionality, authenticity, and love, painting a vibrant picture of the values and behaviors you hope your children will embrace. You understand that you're not just raising children; you're raising future adults, and you are their most influential teacher.

I had the privilege of working at the same school my children attended for preschool through eighth grade. I loved taking them to school and staying there to work. Being on campus with them made me realize that not only was I a role model to them at home, but I was a role model to them at school too. As a school administrator, I knew all the teachers, most of the students and many parents. And all of them knew my children. That meant everything I did could be and often was relayed to my children and then discussed by my kids on our way home from school. It was a great learning experience for me and an opportunity to truly live 24/7 the characteristics and mindsets I most wanted my children to model. Someone was always watching!

As another example of the impact a mom has as a role model, let's take a look at a story about a mom named Linda:

Linda was a dedicated mother to two young children, Ethan and Mia. She loved her kids deeply and always tried to provide them with the best upbringing possible. However, one day, while observing her children's behavior, Linda had a moment of realization that shook her to her core.

Ethan and Mia were playing in the living room, and Linda noticed that they were mimicking her actions and words. Ethan, her son, was pretending to cook in a toy kitchen, just as Linda often did in the real kitchen. Mia, her daughter, was holding a pretend phone to her ear and saying phrases that sounded eerily similar to Linda's conversations with friends.

As Linda watched them, it hit her like a lightning bolt: her children were absorbing everything she said and did. They looked up to her as a role model, and they were learning how to interact with the world by imitating her actions and words. It was a profound and sobering realization.

Watching how her children were acting, Linda knew that she needed to be more aware of her behavior and language in front of them. She understood that every interaction, no matter how seemingly insignificant, could leave a lasting impression on their young minds.

From that moment on, Linda made a conscious effort to model the values and behaviors she wanted her children to embrace. She spoke to them with kindness and respect, even in moments of frustration. She made an effort to use positive language and phrases that encouraged empathy and understanding.

Linda also became more mindful of how she handled stress and conflicts. Instead of reacting impulsively, she took a step back, breathed deeply, and demonstrated problem-solving skills and resilience in front of her children. She wanted them to see that it was okay to face challenges and setbacks and to learn from them.

As the days turned into weeks, Linda noticed a positive change in her children's behavior. They began to exhibit greater kindness, patience, and understanding in their interactions with others. Ethan and Mia also started to express themselves more confidently, knowing that their mother valued their thoughts and opinions.

One evening, as they were having dinner together, Ethan looked at Linda and said, "Mom, I want to be like you when I grow up. You're always so nice and patient."

Linda smiled and nodded her head as she realized the impact of her efforts. "Thank you, Ethan," she replied with a smile. "I want you to know that you inspire me to be the best mom I can be, too."

Linda's journey of self-awareness and mindful parenting continued, but she now had a profound understanding of the responsibility that came with being a role model for her children. She knew that her actions and words had the power to shape their character, values, and future. Linda embraced this role with humility and determination, committed to setting a positive example that would guide her children toward a bright and compassionate future.

As a mom, your actions and behavior significantly impact your child's development. You serve as a role model, influencing their values, behavior, and character. The following are examples of how you can demonstrate being a role model. After each example, you will find three specific actions you can take to model and strengthen your role model mindset. Read through them and choose at least one example that resonates with you. Then, try at least one of the actions and see how it makes you feel. Remember, changing a mindset takes time and the more you practice, the easier it gets.

Demonstrating Respect: Show respect to everyone, regardless of their age, race, gender, or position. Your child will observe and emulate how you treat others, learning to value diversity and equality.
- Kind and Polite Communication: Model polite and respectful communication in your interactions with others, including family members, friends, and strangers. Use "please" and "thank you," and speak in a courteous tone. Your child will learn the importance of treating others with respect through your example.
- Empathy and Understanding: Show empathy and understanding toward others, especially in challenging situations. Discuss how people may have different perspectives or feelings and encourage your child to consider these viewpoints. By demonstrating empathy, you teach your child the value of respecting others' emotions and experiences.
- Conflict Resolution: When conflicts arise, model respectful conflict resolution strategies. Show your child how to express disagreements calmly, listen to the other person's viewpoint, and work together to find solutions that respect everyone's needs and feelings. This teaches your child the importance of resolving conflicts respectfully and peacefully.

MINDSET #6 - ROLE MODELING

<u>Practicing Healthy Habits</u>: Show your child the importance of maintaining a healthy lifestyle. Exercise regularly, eat balanced meals, and ensure adequate sleep. Your child will likely adopt these habits, understanding their importance for overall well-being.

- Regular Exercise: Engage in regular physical activity as a family. Whether it's going for a family walk, bike ride, or playing sports together, make exercise a fun and routine part of your family life. Your child will learn the importance of staying active and maintaining a healthy lifestyle.
- Balanced Nutrition: Model balanced eating habits by preparing and enjoying nutritious meals together. Include a variety of fruits, vegetables, whole grains, and lean proteins in your diet. Explain the importance of making healthy food choices and the benefits it has for their growth and energy.
- Adequate Sleep: Prioritize a consistent sleep schedule for your child and yourself. Ensure that your child gets the recommended amount of sleep for their age. By establishing a bedtime routine and prioritizing adequate rest, you teach your child the value of quality sleep for physical and mental health.

<u>Managing Stress Positively</u>: Life is full of stressors. Show your child how to manage stress in healthy ways, such as through yoga, meditation, or reading. Your child will learn beneficial coping mechanisms for their own life's challenges.

- Practice Mindfulness: Introduce mindfulness techniques to your child by practicing them together. Activities like deep breathing exercises, meditation, or guided relaxation can help both you and your child cope with stress and anxiety in a healthy way.
- Time Management: Show your child how to manage their time effectively and prioritize tasks. Teach them about setting achievable

goals and breaking tasks into smaller, manageable steps. This can help reduce the stress associated with feeling overwhelmed by responsibilities.
- Seek Support and Communication: Encourage open and honest communication about stressors. Model seeking support from friends, family, or professionals when needed. Discuss your own experiences with stress and how you manage it, demonstrating that it's okay to ask for help.

<u>Valuing Education</u>: Show the importance of education by engaging in lifelong learning. Read books, take courses, or learn a new skill. Your child will see the value of continuous learning and personal growth.
- Set High Expectations: Encourage your child to strive for excellence in their studies by setting high but achievable expectations. Emphasize the value of learning and personal growth. When children are held to high expectations, they often rise to meet them, boosting their confidence in their abilities. This fosters a growth mindset where they view challenges as opportunities for development. Over time, they cultivate a strong work ethic, perseverance, and the belief that effort leads to mastery and success.
- Create a Learning-Friendly Environment: Dedicate a quiet and organized space for studying, offer necessary learning materials, and establish a consistent homework routine to foster a positive attitude toward education. This structured learning environment promotes focus and empowers your child to approach their academic endeavors with confidence and enthusiasm.
- Engage in Educational Activities: Participate in educational activities as a family, such as visiting museums, exploring science centers, or reading books together. These experiences demonstrate that learning is not limited to the classroom and can be enjoyable and enriching.

MINDSET #6 - ROLE MODELING

Exhibiting Responsibility: Take responsibility for your actions, admitting when you're wrong and making amends. Your child will learn to be accountable for their actions, an essential trait for personal and professional relationships.

- Set and Follow Through on Commitments: When you make commitments or promises, ensure that you follow through on them consistently. Whether it's completing tasks around the house or fulfilling work obligations, your reliability serves as a powerful example.
- Organize and Plan: Demonstrate effective organization and planning skills in your daily life. Use calendars, to-do lists, and time management techniques to stay on top of responsibilities. Involve your child in age-appropriate planning and organizing tasks. By witnessing and participating in structured organization and planning, your child develops essential life skills, fostering a sense of responsibility, enhancing their problem-solving capabilities, and preparing them for future independence and success.
- Accountability for Mistakes: Show your child that taking responsibility for mistakes is a sign of maturity. If you make an error, admit it openly, discuss how to rectify the situation and emphasize the importance of learning from mistakes.

Handling Finances Wisely: Teach your child the importance of financial responsibility. Budget wisely, save for the future, and make thoughtful spending decisions. Your child will develop a healthy understanding of money management.

- Budgeting Together: Involve your child in the budgeting process. Sit down together to create a weekly budget that outlines income, expenses, and savings goals. This helps your child understand the importance of managing money effectively.

- Smart Spending Choices: When making purchases, explain your thought process behind spending decisions. Emphasize the difference between needs and wants, and discuss the value of saving money for future goals.
- Savings Routine: Establish a weekly savings routine. Encourage your child to set aside a portion of their allowance or earnings for savings. Discuss the benefits of saving, such as financial security and achieving long-term goals.

<u>Practicing Kindness and Empathy</u>: Show kindness and empathy to others. Volunteer, help a neighbor, or comfort a friend in need. Your child will learn the value of compassion and kindness in making the world a better place.

- Random Acts of Kindness: Encourage your child to perform random acts of kindness, such as helping a friend, offering a compliment, or sharing with others. Participate in these acts together to show that kindness is a value worth practicing. Engaging in and witnessing acts of kindness cultivates compassion, boosts your child's self-esteem, and nurtures a strong sense of community and interconnectedness, teaching them the joy and importance of giving and caring for others.
- Empathetic Listening: Teach your child the importance of empathetic listening. When they share their thoughts and feelings, model active listening by showing understanding and asking questions to clarify their emotions. Learning empathetic listening enhances your child's emotional intelligence, fosters deeper connections with others, and equips them with the invaluable skill of understanding and valuing different perspectives and emotions.
- Volunteer Together: Engage in volunteer activities as a family. Participating in community service or charitable work provides real-world examples of empathy and kindness in action.

MINDSET #6 - ROLE MODELING

<u>Nurturing Relationships</u>: Show your child how to nurture and maintain relationships. Spend quality time with family and friends, resolving conflicts in a healthy manner. Your child will learn to value relationships and communication skills.

- Quality Time: Dedicate quality time to spend with your loved ones. Engage in activities you all enjoy, have meaningful conversations, and create shared memories. Being present and fully engaged during these moments strengthens bonds.
- Open Communication: Foster open and honest communication within your relationships. Encourage everyone to express their thoughts, feelings, and concerns. Actively listen and show empathy to create a safe space for sharing.
- Support and Appreciation: Show support and appreciation for one another regularly. Offer encouragement, express gratitude, and celebrate each other's achievements and milestones. These actions reinforce the value of your relationships.

<u>Pursuing Passions</u>: Show your child the importance of pursuing passions. Engage in your hobbies or interests and encourage them to explore theirs. They'll learn the importance of personal fulfillment and joy.

- Set Goals: Help your child identify their passions and interests, and then guide them in setting achievable goals related to those passions. Encourage them to break these goals down into smaller, manageable steps. Goal-setting empowers your child with direction, motivation, and a clear sense of purpose, fostering self-confidence and determination in their pursuits.
- Allocate Time: Dedicate time to pursue passions regularly. Create a schedule that allows your child to engage in activities, hobbies, or learning experiences related to their passions. Show your support by providing the necessary resources and opportunities. Regularly

allocating time nurtures your child's commitment, cultivates discipline, and ensures continuous growth and development in their areas of interest.
- Model Passion Pursuit: Be a role model by actively pursuing your own passions and interests. Share your experiences, challenges, and successes with your child. This demonstrates that the pursuit of passions is a lifelong endeavor.

Modeling Honesty and Integrity: Uphold honesty and integrity in all you do. Be truthful, keep your promises, and uphold your values. Your child will learn to value honesty and integrity, essential for trust and respect in their relationships.
- Truthfulness: Always be truthful in your words and actions, even when it's challenging. Explain the importance of honesty and how it builds trust in relationships.
- Consistency: Align your actions with your values and principles consistently. Show that you do what you say you will do and follow through on commitments. Observing consistent behavior instills trust, teaches the importance of reliability, and models integrity in personal and interpersonal relationships.
- Accountability: If you make a mistake or wrong someone, take responsibility for your actions. Apologize when necessary and make amends, illustrating the value of integrity and accountability.

Practicing Self-Love and Acceptance: Teach your child about self-love and acceptance by embracing your body, mind, and spirit. Show them it's okay to love yourself as you are, with all your strengths and weaknesses. This will help them develop a healthy body image and self-esteem.
- Positive Self-Talk: Model positive self-talk by using affirming language when discussing yourself. Avoid self-criticism and

demonstrate self-compassion. Encourage your child to do the same.
- Healthy Self-Care: Prioritize self-care activities that promote physical and emotional well-being. Show your child that taking time for relaxation, exercise, and self-nurturing is an essential part of a balanced and fulfilling life.
- Celebrate Uniqueness: Embrace and celebrate your child's unique qualities and interests. Encourage them to explore their passions and talents, fostering a sense of self-worth and confidence.

<u>Advocating for Yourself and Others</u>: Stand up for your rights and for those who can't stand up for themselves. This shows your child the importance of fairness and justice, teaching them to be empathetic and socially responsible.
- Assertive Communication: Teach your child how to express their needs, concerns, and opinions assertively, politely and respectfully. Encourage them to use "I" statements to communicate their feelings and advocate for what they believe is right.
- Stand Up Against Injustice: Model standing up against injustice or unfair treatment. Discuss real-world examples and encourage your child to voice their concerns when they witness wrongdoing or discrimination.
- Empathy and Support: Encourage empathy and support for others who may not have a voice. Teach your child to listen to others' perspectives and advocate on behalf of those who may be marginalized or facing difficulties.

<u>Being Resourceful</u>: Solve problems creatively and use resources wisely. This will teach your child resilience, adaptability, and the importance of being resourceful.
- Problem-Solving Together: Involve your child in problem-solving activities. When facing challenges or obstacles, discuss possible

solutions together and encourage them to brainstorm ideas. This fosters a resourceful mindset.
- Encourage Independence: Give your child opportunities to tackle tasks on their own. Allow them to make decisions and find solutions independently, even if it means making mistakes along the way.
- Model Resourcefulness: Demonstrate resourcefulness in your own life by efficiently using available resources, adapting to changing circumstances, and finding innovative solutions to everyday problems. Observing resourcefulness equips your child with the resilience, creativity, and adaptability needed to navigate challenges effectively.

Expressing Gratitude: Regularly express gratitude for the good things in your life. This will help your child develop a positive mindset and appreciate the blessings in their life.
- Modeling Gratitude in Difficult Times: Even when facing hardships or disappointments, verbalize something you are thankful for, showing your children that there's always a silver lining. Observing gratitude even in tough situations equips your children with resilience, teaching them to shift their focus from what's lacking or challenging to what's abundant and supportive in their lives.
- Acknowledging Non-Material Blessings: Beyond giving thanks to those responsible for gifts or tangible acts of kindness, make it a habit to express gratitude for intangible blessings like love, health, family bonding moments, or a beautiful day. By appreciating non-material blessings, your children learn to value deeper emotional and experiential aspects of life, fostering a holistic sense of gratitude that goes beyond possessions.
- Thank-You Notes: After birthdays or special occasions, have your children write thank-you notes or draw thank-you pictures for the

gifts or acts of kindness they've received. Having your children create personalized thank-you notes provides them with a tangible way to express their appreciation, underscoring the significance of putting in the effort to demonstrate gratitude and fostering their ability to communicate thoughtfully.

<u>Balancing Work and Life</u>: Show your child how you manage your career and personal life. This will teach them about responsibility, time management, and the importance of maintaining a healthy work-life balance.
- Establish Boundaries: Ensure that you designate specific times for work and family. For instance, if you're working from home, set clear start and end times for your workday and communicate this to your children, making sure you disconnect from work tasks when it's family time. When your children see you maintaining clear boundaries between work and family time, they learn the importance of compartmentalizing and dedicating quality time to personal relationships, fostering a healthy work-life equilibrium.
- Prioritize Self-Care: Set aside moments in your week dedicated to self-care, whether it's a hobby, exercise, or simply relaxation, and share this practice with your children, perhaps by organizing family self-care moments like movie nights or outdoor outings. Observing and participating in regular self-care activities teaches your children the value of personal well-being, emphasizing that taking breaks and rejuvenating is vital to maintaining a balanced life.
- Involve Children in Task Management: Create a visual family calendar or to-do list where you plot out work commitments and family activities. Occasionally, sit down with your children to discuss and organize the week, highlighting how you're juggling both spheres. Engaging with a shared task management system exposes

your children to proactive planning, showing them firsthand how thoughtful organization helps achieve a harmonious balance between professional and personal commitments.

Practicing Patience: Display patience in challenging situations. Your child will observe your calm and composed demeanor in stressful situations, and learn to do the same.
- Count to Ten: When you feel impatience rising, pause and count to ten slowly in your mind before reacting. This brief moment of mindfulness can help you regain composure and respond more calmly.
- Take Deep Breaths: Inhale deeply through your nose and exhale slowly through your mouth. Repeat this breathing exercise a few times. It can help reduce stress and frustration, allowing you to be more patient.
- Practice Active Listening: When engaged in a conversation, focus on truly listening to the other person without interrupting or formulating your response immediately. Give them your full attention, which requires patience and respect for their perspective.

Being Environmentally Conscious: Practice and teach environmentally friendly habits like recycling, conserving water, and reducing waste. This will teach your child the importance of caring for the planet.
- Reduce, Reuse, Recycle: Follow the "3 Rs" to minimize waste. Reduce consumption by buying only what you need, reuse items when possible, and recycle materials like paper, plastic, glass, and aluminum.
- Conserve Energy: Reduce energy consumption by turning off lights, appliances, and electronics when not in use. Invest in energy-efficient appliances and use programmable thermostats to save on heating and cooling costs.

- Use Renewable Energy: If feasible, switch to renewable energy sources like solar or wind power to reduce your reliance on fossil fuels.

Being a Good Listener: Show your child that you're interested in what they have to say by actively listening to them. This teaches them the importance of communication and respect for others' thoughts and feelings.
- Ask Open-Ended Questions: Encourage the speaker to share more by asking open-ended questions that require more than a simple "yes" or "no" response. This demonstrates your interest in their thoughts.
- Be Present: Be mentally present as well as physically. Avoid thinking about what you'll say next or unrelated matters. Stay in the moment to fully absorb the speaker's words.
- Use Nonverbal Cues: Use nonverbal cues such as nodding, smiling, or using facial expressions to show that you are actively listening and engaged in the conversation.

Fostering Independence: Encourage your child to do things on their own, even if they make mistakes. This will help your child become confident, self-reliant, and learn to take responsibility for their actions.
- Encourage Decision-Making: When appropriate let your children make decisions for themselves, even if it means they may make mistakes. Offer guidance and support, but let them experience the consequences of their choices, as this helps them learn and develop decision-making skills.
- Provide Opportunities for Learning: Offer opportunities for your child to acquire new skills and knowledge. This might involve providing resources, training, or mentorship. Empower them to take the initiative in their own learning and development.
- Promote Self-Responsibility: Encourage your child to take

responsibility for their actions and commitments. Help them set goals and priorities, and hold them accountable for meeting these objectives. Encourage self-discipline and time management.

Exhibiting Perseverance: When facing obstacles, don't give up easily. Show your child that perseverance is key in achieving goals, teaching them not to fear failures but see them as opportunities to learn and grow.

- Know Where You Want to Go: Define your objectives and establish a clear vision of what you want to achieve and how you are going to get there. Having specific, measurable goals gives you a sense of purpose and direction. Break these goals into smaller, manageable steps to make progress more achievable.
- Stay Committed: Perseverance often requires a strong commitment to your goals, even when faced with obstacles or setbacks. Maintain your dedication and remind yourself why your goals are important to you. This sense of purpose can help you push through difficult times.
- Learn from Failure: Understand that setbacks and failures are a natural part of any journey. Instead of giving up when you encounter obstacles, view them as opportunities to learn and grow. Analyze what went wrong, adjust your approach, and continue forward with newfound knowledge and resilience.

***

By demonstrating these behaviors through your actions, you teach your child vital life skills and values. Actions often speak louder than words, and your children are always watching, learning, and mirroring your behaviors. Your role as a role model is crucial in shaping your children's character and values. The values and behaviors you model play a pivotal role in defining who they are and their view of the world. Your role as a mom goes beyond care giving; you are their first teacher and greatest example.

Chapter Summary

- **You are Your Child's Role Model:** Recognize your profound impact as a role model. Strive to embody the values you wish to instill in your children, such as kindness, honesty, perseverance, and respect. Your children will imitate what they see you do.

- **The Silent Language of Parenting:** Understand that role modeling is a non-verbal yet powerful form of communication. Your actions, attitudes, and behaviors constantly convey messages to your children.

- **Take Advantage of Daily Opportunities for Modeling Values:** Embrace each day as an opportunity to demonstrate core values through your actions. Show kindness, honesty, perseverance and respect in your everyday interactions.

- **Teach Resilience and Accountability:** Model how to handle challenges and mistakes. Demonstrate resilience, patience, and grace under pressure, teaching your children that mistakes are opportunities for growth.

- **Model Healthy Habits and Self-Care:** Show the importance of physical health, stress management, and personal well-being. Your habits set the foundation for your children's lifelong health and lifestyle choices.

- **Respect Individuality:** Celebrate your children's unique traits and interests, encouraging them to become the best versions of themselves, rather than mini versions of you.

• **Show Authenticity in Role Modeling:** Admit faults, apologize when necessary, and share your struggles. This authenticity models humility and the human aspect of adulthood.

• **Living Lessons for Life:** Navigate your role as a role model with intentionality, authenticity, and love. Understand that your actions shape your children's future behaviors, values, and character development.

• **You are Your Child's Most Influential Teacher:** Recognize that your role goes beyond caregiving. You are your children's first and most influential teacher, shaping their character and worldview through your everyday actions and behaviors.

Chapter 12

Mindset #7 - Self-Care

The Importance of Taking Care of Yourself So You Can Be An Unstoppable Mom

"Taking care of myself doesn't mean 'Me First', it means 'Me too'."
- L.R. Knosts

Motherhood embodies a profound expression of love, nurturing, and care. While the focus is often on the well-being of your children, an important practice that helps you be the best you can be is the practice of self-care. Recognizing the sage wisdom in the saying, "You can't pour from an empty cup," unstoppable mothers understand that they need to attend to their physical and emotional needs to sustain the energy and mental resilience required to care for others.

The concept of self-care goes beyond the indulgence of a spa day or an occasional night out. It encompasses the nurturing of your physical, emotional, and mental well-being. It involves regular exercise, a balanced diet, adequate rest, and regular medical check-ups. It also includes attending to your emotional health through stress management, pursuing hobbies, connecting with friends, or seeking professional help when needed.

An unstoppable mom acknowledges that self-care isn't selfish but

MINDSET #7 - SELF-CARE

rather a necessity. It is about preserving health and happiness, which in turn, enables you to be the best parent you can be. When you acknowledge that taking care of your own needs is an essential part of your role as a caregiver - when you are healthy and content - you are better equipped to provide the support and care your children require.

A significant aspect of self-care is also the recognition and acceptance of your emotional state. Motherhood can elicit a broad range of emotions, some joyous and some stressful. It's crucial as a mom to allow yourself to feel these emotions, process them, and seek support when needed. Whether it's sharing experiences with friends, discussing concerns with your partner, or seeking professional guidance, these emotional outlets contribute significantly to a mom's emotional well-being.

Practicing self-care also sets a powerful example for your children. When children observe you, their mom, prioritizing your health and well-being, they learn the importance of self-care. They understand that personal health and happiness are vital for overall success and well-being. By practicing self-care, a mom not only enhances her own life but also imparts a valuable life lesson to her children.

Additionally, self-care plays a crucial role in building resilience. The journey of motherhood comes with its fair share of challenges and stressors. Regular self-care activities can provide a much-needed breather, helping to recharge, rejuvenate and build resilience. This resilience is essential in navigating the highs and lows of motherhood and ensuring that the journey, despite its challenges, remains fulfilling and enjoyable.

Self-care is not something that comes easy to me. I often feel like I have so much to do, I don't have time for self-care. But I also have learned over the years that it is extremely important for me to take care of myself just like I take care of my children and husband. And I know that a little down time can go a long, long way. A fifteen-minute walk, thirty minutes to read my favorite author's newest release or an evening watching a Hallmark movie can refresh me like nothing else. Find what it is that you enjoy doing and make sure you make the time to do it on a regular basis. Your family will appreciate the relaxed new you as much as you do.

Self-care is an indispensable part of being an unstoppable mom. It is the underpinning factor that ensures you can sustain the physical energy and mental resilience needed to provide the best care for your children. By prioritizing self-care, you nurture your own well-being, set a positive example for your children, and enhance your capacity to navigate the fascinating journey of motherhood. It is so true - a happy, healthy mom is the cornerstone of a happy, healthy family.

As an example of the importance of self-care, especially for moms, let us take a look at a story about a mom named Krista:

Krista was a devoted wife and mother of two wonderful children. She took immense pride in her role as the heart of her family and worked tirelessly to meet their needs. However, in her pursuit of being the best wife and mother she could be, Krista often neglected one vital aspect of her life—self-care.

Her days were a whirlwind of responsibilities, from managing the household to helping the kids with their homework, and from cooking dinner to tucking them into bed. It was a routine that left Krista feeling exhausted and drained, but she rarely allowed herself the luxury of self-care.

One day, Krista's husband, David, noticed the toll that this non-stop routine was taking on his wife. He could see the weariness in her eyes and the way she seemed to be running on empty. He knew that Krista needed a break and some time to focus on herself.

David decided to gently push Krista to indulge in self-care. He suggested that she take a weekend off to do something she loved, whether it was going for a spa day, enjoying a favorite hobby, or simply spending time with friends. At first, Krista was hesitant and felt guilty for even considering it, but David was persistent.

Eventually, Krista agreed to take a weekend away for herself. She booked a cozy cabin in the woods, far away from the daily responsibilities that had been consuming her. As she packed her bags and prepared to leave, her children, Lily and Max, looked at her with curiosity.

"Mom, are you really going away?" Lily asked.

Krista nodded and smiled. "Just for a little while. Mom needs some time to rest and recharge so that I can be the best mommy for you when I come back."

The weekend turned out to be a revelation for Krista. She spent her days hiking, reading, and simply enjoying the tranquility of nature. She realized that taking care of herself wasn't selfish; it was essential for her well-being and her ability to care for her family.

When Krista returned home, she felt like a different person. She was more rested, relaxed, and content. Her children noticed the change immediately. Lily and Max saw their mom's smile return, and they could sense her new found energy and positivity.

One evening, as they were all sitting down for dinner, Lily spoke up, "Mom, you seem so much happier now. I like it when you're not so tired all the time."

Krista looked at her family and realized the profound impact that self-care had on her life and her ability to be there for her loved ones. "I'm glad you noticed," she said. "Taking care of myself helps me take better care of all of you. It's important for us to find a balance."

David nodded in agreement, grateful to see his wife finally embracing self-care. Krista had learned that caring for herself wasn't selfish—it was an act of love that allowed her to be the best wife and mother she could be. From that day forward, she made self-care a priority in her life, knowing that it was an investment in the well-being and happiness of her family as well.

Self-care is crucial for moms as it allows you to recharge and maintain your physical, emotional, and mental well-being. The following are examples of how you can practice self-care. After each example, you will find three specific actions you can take to model and strengthen your self-care mindset. Read through them and choose at least one example that resonates with you. Then, try at least one of the actions and see how it makes you feel. Remember, changing a mindset takes time and the more you practice, the easier it gets.

<u>Physical Exercise</u>: Regular physical exercise such as jogging, yoga, dancing, or even a brisk walk can enhance physical well-being and elevate mood.
- Take Short Walks: Whenever you have a break or a spare moment, go for a brisk walk, even if it's just around your office or home. A 10-15 minute walk can boost your mood, increase energy levels, and improve your overall physical health.
- Practice Quick Workouts: Dedicate 10-15 minutes to a quick, at-home workout routine. You can do bodyweight exercises like squats, push-ups, or planks to get your heart rate up and improve strength and flexibility.
- Use Active Transportation: Whenever possible, choose active modes of transportation like walking or cycling for short trips instead of driving. It's a great way to incorporate physical activity into your daily routine.

<u>Healthy Eating</u>: Prioritizing a balanced, nutritious diet is a key part of self-care. It's essential for maintaining good health and energy levels.
- Mindful Eating: Take a few minutes before each meal to pause, breathe, and reflect on your food choices. Pay attention to the flavors, textures,

MINDSET #7 - SELF-CARE

and smells of your food. Eating mindfully can help you savor your meals and prevent overeating.
- Hydration: Keep a reusable water bottle with you and make it a habit to drink water throughout the day. Staying hydrated is essential for overall health and can also help curb unnecessary snacking.
- Plan Balanced Snacks: Prepare healthy snacks in advance, such as cut-up fruits, vegetables, or a small handful of nuts. Having these readily available can help you make nutritious choices when you're hungry between meals.

Adequate Rest: Moms often sacrifice their sleep for their children, but adequate sleep is essential for overall health and energy levels. Power naps, early nights, or sleeping in when possible can all contribute to better rest.
- Establish a Consistent Sleep Schedule: Try to go to bed and wake up at the same time every day, even on weekends. This helps regulate your body's internal clock, making it easier to fall asleep and wake up feeling refreshed.
- Create a Relaxing Bedtime Routine: Develop a calming routine before bedtime to signal to your body that it's time to wind down. Activities like reading, taking a warm bath, or practicing relaxation techniques can help prepare your mind and body for sleep.
- Create a Comfortable Sleep Environment: Ensure your sleep space is conducive to rest. Keep your bedroom dark, quiet, and at a comfortable temperature. Invest in a comfortable mattress and pillows that support restful sleep.

Mindfulness and Meditation: Practices like mindfulness, meditation, or deep-breathing exercises can help manage stress and promote a sense of calm and well-being.

- Take a 5-Minute Breathing Break: Set aside a few minutes each day to focus on your breath. Find a quiet space, sit comfortably, and close your eyes. Take slow, deep breaths, paying attention to the sensation of the breath entering and leaving your body. This brief mindfulness exercise can help you center yourself and reduce stress.
- Practice Gratitude Meditation: Spend a few minutes each day reflecting on things you're grateful for. This can be done in the morning or before bed. Simply list or think about three things you're thankful for, savoring each one. Gratitude meditation can enhance your overall sense of well-being.
- Morning Meditation Routine: Begin your day with a short meditation session, inviting your children to join. Use this time to focus on your breath, set intentions for the day, or practice gratitude together. Witnessing and participating in daily meditation helps your children understand the value of starting the day with clarity and intention, introducing them to tools for emotional regulation and present-moment awareness.

<u>Pursuing a Hobby</u>: Whether it's reading, gardening, painting, or any other activity that brings joy, having a hobby can provide a therapeutic and fulfilling outlet.
- Set Aside Dedicated Time: Allocate a specific, short block of time each day or week to engage in your hobby. Even if it's just 15-30 minutes, this dedicated time allows you to focus on your passion and provides a break from daily stressors.
- Create a Relaxing Environment: Make your hobby time a serene and enjoyable experience. Set up a cozy space with the necessary materials or equipment. Play calming music or light scented candles to enhance the atmosphere.
- Immerse Yourself Fully: When you engage in your hobby, give it your full attention. Let go of worries or distractions and allow yourself to

be fully present in the activity. This mindfulness can help you relax and find joy in your hobby.

<u>Time with Friends</u>: Maintaining social connections is important for emotional health. Regularly catching up with friends, either in person or virtually, can provide a refreshing break.
- Plan Regular Check-Ins: Schedule brief but regular check-ins with friends, even if they're virtual or by phone. A short call or message to catch up and share updates can help maintain your connections and strengthen your friendships.
- Meet for a Quick Coffee or Meal: Invite a friend for a short coffee break or a quick lunch or dinner. Even a brief in-person or virtual meet-up can provide a sense of connection and offer a break from daily routines.
- Send a Thoughtful Message: Take a moment to send a heartfelt message to a friend expressing appreciation or letting them know you're thinking of them. Small gestures like this can go a long way in maintaining and nurturing friendships.

<u>Professional Care</u>: Regular medical check-ups, massages, therapy sessions, or even a trip to a beauty salon are important aspects of self-care that moms should not neglect.
- Schedule Regular Check-Ups: Prioritize your physical health by scheduling regular check-ups with healthcare professionals. This includes routine visits to your primary care physician, dentist, eye doctor, and any specialists you may need based on your health needs.
- Seek Mental Health Support: If you're experiencing mental health challenges, don't hesitate to reach out to a mental health professional. Schedule an initial consultation or therapy session to discuss your concerns and explore treatment options.
- Invest in Skill Development: Consider professional development or

coaching to enhance your skills and advance in your career. Seeking guidance from mentors or career counselors can help you set and achieve professional goals.

Personal Growth: Attending workshops, taking an online course, or engaging in activities that contribute to personal growth and skills can be rewarding and empowering.

- Set Clear Objectives: Define specific, achievable goals that align with your interests, values, and aspirations. Whether they're related to career, relationships, health, or personal development, having clear objectives provides direction and motivation for growth.
- Continuously Learn: Cultivate a habit of lifelong learning. Read books, take courses, attend workshops, or engage in online learning platforms to acquire new knowledge and skills. Learning keeps your mind active and adaptable.
- Step Out of Your Comfort Zone: Growth often occurs when you challenge yourself and embrace discomfort. Take calculated risks, try new experiences, and confront your fears. These actions can expand your capabilities and boost self-confidence.

Quiet Time: Sometimes, you may just need a few quiet moments to yourself. This could involve a peaceful morning coffee, a solitary walk, or simply sitting in silence for a few minutes.

- Create a Daily Ritual: Set aside a few minutes each day for quiet time. Find a peaceful spot where you won't be disturbed, whether it's in your home, a park, or a quiet corner of your workplace. Dedicate this time to silence, reflection, or meditation.
- Practice Mindfulness: Use your quiet time to engage in mindfulness exercises. Focus on your breath and sensations in your body, or simply observe your thoughts without judgment. This can help you become more present and reduce stress.

MINDSET #7 - SELF-CARE

- Disconnect from Technology: During your quiet time, disconnect from digital devices. Turn off your phone, computer, and any other electronic distractions to create a truly peaceful and uninterrupted environment.

Setting Boundaries: Moms can practice self-care by setting boundaries. This could mean saying "no" when overwhelmed, delegating tasks, or carving out 'me time' regularly.

- Identify Your Needs and Limits: Reflect on your own needs, values, and limits. Consider what makes you feel comfortable or uncomfortable in various situations or relationships. Being self-aware is the first step in setting boundaries that align with your well-being.
- Communicate Clearly and Assertively: When you identify a need for boundaries, communicate them clearly and assertively to the people involved. Use "I" statements to express your feelings and needs, and be firm but respectful in your communication.
- Enforce Boundaries Consistently: Once you've established boundaries, it's crucial to enforce them consistently. This means taking action if your boundaries are violated. Depending on the situation, this might involve assertive communication, distancing yourself from the person or situation, or seeking support from a trusted friend or therapist.

Emotional Expression: Allowing yourself to feel and express emotions, whether through journaling, talking with a trusted friend or partner, or even therapy, can be a powerful form of self-care.

- Identify Your Emotions: Practice self-awareness by identifying and labeling your emotions. Pay attention to what you're feeling and why. Journaling can be a helpful tool for exploring and understanding your emotions.

- Express Emotions Clearly: Communicate your emotions clearly and honestly with others. Use "I" statements to express how you feel and what you need. For example, say, "I feel hurt when you cancel our plans without notice. I need more consistency in our communication."
- Choose Appropriate Outlets: Find healthy outlets for your emotions. This might include talking to a trusted friend or family member, seeking support from a therapist, or engaging in creative activities like art, music, or writing to express yourself.

Digital Detox: Spending some time away from screens and social media can help reduce stress and promote better sleep. This could be for an hour before bedtime, a particular day of the week, or even a weekend.

- Set Clear Boundaries: Establish specific rules and timeframes for your digital detox. Decide when and for how long you will disconnect from electronic devices. Start with short periods, like a few hours or a day, and gradually extend the duration as you become more comfortable with the practice.
- Plan Alternative Activities: Identify offline activities that you enjoy and can engage in during your digital detox. This might include reading a physical book, going for a walk, practicing a hobby, or spending quality time with loved ones. Having alternative activities in mind can make it easier to resist the temptation of digital devices.
- Notify Contacts: If you're disconnecting for an extended period, inform friends, family, or colleagues in advance so they know you won't be readily available online. Set up an automated email response or social media message to let people know you're on a digital detox and provide alternative ways to reach you in case of emergencies.

Spending Time in Nature: Taking a walk in a park, gardening, hiking, or simply sitting in a natural setting can help reduce stress and boost mood.

- Plan Regular Outdoor Activities: Schedule regular outdoor activities like hiking, biking, picnics, or nature walks. Set aside specific times in your calendar to ensure you prioritize these experiences.
- Unplug and Be Present: When you're in nature, disconnect from digital devices and distractions. Use this time to immerse yourself in the natural world, be present in the moment, and engage your senses. Pay attention to the sights, sounds, smells, and sensations around you.
- Practice Mindfulness: Incorporate mindfulness into your nature outings by practicing deep breathing, meditation, or simply sitting quietly and observing the environment. This can help you relax and deepen your connection with nature.

<u>Practicing Gratitude</u>: Maintaining a gratitude journal or simply taking a few moments each day to acknowledge the things you are grateful for can improve mental well-being and provide a more positive outlook.

- Keep a Gratitude Journal: Dedicate a few minutes each day to write down things you're grateful for. It could be as simple as a beautiful sunset, a kind gesture from a friend, or a personal achievement. Regularly reflecting on the positive aspects of your life can foster a more optimistic mindset.
- Express Gratitude to Others: Take the time to thank the people in your life. Send a heartfelt message, write a thank-you note, or express your appreciation verbally. Letting others know you're grateful for their presence or actions not only benefits them but also strengthens your relationships.
- Practice Mindfulness of Gratitude: During moments of quiet or meditation, focus on gratitude. Reflect on the things you appreciate in your life and the positive experiences you've had. Cultivate a sense of gratitude in the present moment.

Taking a Bath or Shower: This may seem basic, but a long, relaxing bath or a refreshing shower can do wonders for your mood and gives you some much-needed alone time.

- Create a Relaxing Atmosphere: Set the mood by creating a soothing atmosphere in your bathroom. Dim the lights, light scented candles, or play calming music to enhance the relaxation experience. Make your bathing area a sanctuary for relaxation.
- Use Aromatherapy: Incorporate aromatherapy into your bath or shower routine by using scented bath salts, essential oils, or shower gels with calming fragrances like lavender or eucalyptus. The soothing scents can help reduce stress and anxiety.
- Practice Mindfulness: Use this time to be present and mindful. Pay attention to the sensations of the water on your skin, the scent of your bath products, and the warmth or coolness of the water. Let go of any stressful thoughts and focus on the sensory experience.

Listening to Music or Podcasts: Whether it's uplifting music, calming classical tunes, or an engaging podcast, listening to something you enjoy can be a great way to relax and recharge.

- Curate Playlists: Create playlists of your favorite songs or podcasts that align with your current mood or goals. For example, you can have playlists for relaxation, motivation, and specific activities like workouts or cooking. Having these playlists ready allows you to easily access the content you need.
- Dedicate Time for Listening: Set aside specific times for music or podcast listening. Whether it's during your morning commute, while doing household chores, or as part of your wind-down routine before bed, dedicating time ensures you prioritize this self-care activity.
- Explore New Content: Occasionally, step out of your comfort zone and explore new genres, artists, or podcasts. Discovering new content

MINDSET #7 - SELF-CARE

can be exciting and broaden your horizons. It can also provide fresh perspectives and inspiration.

<u>Investing in Comfort</u>: Investing in things that make you feel comfortable can be a form of self-care. This could be a comfy pair of shoes, a cozy blanket, or a good-quality mattress.

- Create a Cozy Space: Design a comfortable and inviting environment in your home. Invest in cozy furniture, soft blankets, plush pillows, and soothing lighting to make your living spaces warm and welcoming. This will create a retreat where you can relax and unwind.
- Choose Comfortable Clothing: Invest in comfortable clothing made from soft, breathable materials. Whether it's lounge wear, pajamas, or everyday attire, wearing comfortable clothing can significantly enhance your comfort and overall well-being.
- Prioritize Self-Care: Allocate time in your schedule for self-care activities that bring you comfort and relaxation. Whether it's a warm bath, a massage, a favorite book, or a soothing cup of tea, make self-care a regular part of your routine.

<u>Spending Time with Pets</u>: If you have pets, spending time with them can be therapeutic and stress-relieving.

- Quality Playtime: Dedicate a portion of your day to engaging in interactive play with your pet. Whether it's playing fetch, hide-and-seek, or simply cuddling on the couch, quality playtime strengthens your bond and provides mental and physical stimulation for your pet.
- Outdoor Adventures: Take your pet on outdoor adventures like walks, hikes, or trips to the park. These outings not only offer exercise for both you and your pet but also allow you to connect with nature and enjoy the fresh air.
- Mindful Presence: Practice mindfulness while spending time with

your pet. Pay close attention to their behavior, body language, and the simple joy they bring to your life. This mindful presence can deepen your connection and bring you both a sense of contentment.

Engaging in Spiritual Practices: If you're spiritually inclined, practices like prayer, attending a religious service, or studying spiritual texts can be comforting and grounding.
- Set Aside Time for Spiritual Activities: Dedicate a specific time each day or week for your spiritual practice. This might involve meditation, prayer, reading sacred texts, or participating in religious or spiritual rituals. Consistency can help you build a deeper connection to your practice.
- Reflect and Journal: After your spiritual practice, take a moment to reflect on your thoughts, feelings, and insights. Consider keeping a spiritual journal to record your experiences, questions, and moments of inspiration.
- Join a Community: Seek out like-minded individuals by joining a spiritual or religious community or group. Engaging with others who share your beliefs can provide support, a sense of belonging, and opportunities for deeper exploration of your spiritual path.

Learning Something New: This can be as simple as trying a new recipe, or as involved as learning a new language. The process of learning can be engaging and rewarding, and can help you feel more accomplished and self-confident.
- Set Clear Learning Goals: Define what you want to learn and why it matters to you. Having clear goals and a sense of purpose can motivate you to stay committed to your learning journey.
- Establish a Learning Routine: Dedicate regular time for learning in your schedule. It could be a few minutes each day or longer

sessions on specific days of the week, depending on your availability. Consistency is key to making progress.
- Embrace Diverse Learning Methods: Explore different ways of learning, such as reading books, taking online courses, watching educational videos, or participating in hands-on experiences. Variety can make the learning process more engaging and enjoyable.

***

Self-care is not selfish. It's necessary. It makes you more positive, patient, resilient, and better able to care for your children. It's about maintaining and keeping your own cup full so you can give to others.

The key to self-care is finding what works best for you. It's not about grand gestures or expensive treats, but about small, regular acts that help you maintain your well-being. It's important to remember that self-care is not a luxury, but a necessity. It is not something to feel guilty about.

So, what do you enjoy doing?
- Reading a book
- Watching a Rom-Com (Hallmark movies? Oh yeah!)
- Hiking
- Taking a class
- Going to a movie
- Eating out
- Dancing
- Playing a sport
- Joining a club
- Taking a nap

Whatever it is, make sure you make the time to do what you enjoy and do it often. It's good for you and good for your family.

Chapter Summary

- **Self-Care is Essential, Not Selfish:** It's crucial to understand that self-care is necessary, not a luxury. It helps you stay positive, patient, and resilient, enabling you to provide better care for your children.

- **Keep Your Cup Full:** Practicing self-care is about keeping your own cup full so you can give to others. It's not just about pampering yourself occasionally, but about consistently attending to your own needs.

- **Find What Works for You:** Self-care doesn't have to be about grand gestures or expensive treats. It's about small, regular acts that help you maintain your well-being.

- **Allow Yourself to Have Guilt-Free Self-Care:** Taking time for yourself is not something to feel guilty about. It's a necessary part of being a healthy, happy mom.

- **Identify Activities You Enjoy:** Identify activities you enjoy, whether it's reading, watching movies, hiking, taking classes, eating out, dancing, playing sports, joining clubs, or even taking naps.

- **Schedule Your Self-Care Activities:** Make sure to regularly include the activities you enjoy in your busy schedule. It's beneficial for you and, by extension, good for your family.

Chapter 13

Harnessing the Power of the 7 Mindsets

Unleash the Unstoppable Mom in You

> *"Mothers are like glue. Even when you can't see them, they're still holding the family together.*
> - Susan Gale

In the symphony of life, there's a unique tune that resonates with strength, love, and infinite patience - the tune of motherhood. As we approach the last chapter of Be an Unstoppable Mom, let's pause for a moment of reflection.

In the chapters of this book, you've journeyed through the seven powerful mindsets that don't just define the modern mom but are a testament to the indomitable spirit of motherhood across the ages. These seven mindsets are not merely concepts; they are transformative tools, powerful reminders of the strength you possess. They are the very heartbeat of a mother's indomitable spirit, the unwavering strength that propels you forward, day in and day out.

These mindsets are:
- Growth
- Positivity
- Patience and Understanding
- Unconditional Love

- Mindful Presence
- Role Modeling
- Self-Care

As we do a quick review of the seven mindsets, keep in mind that "success" in motherhood isn't one-size-fits-all. Every family, every child, and every mom is different. What matters most is that your children feel loved, nurtured, and guided in a way that helps them develop into their best selves where they are confident, caring, and resilient.

It's also important to note that no mom is perfect and every mom has her challenging days - an unstoppable mom understands this, too. Employing one or many of these seven mindsets will help you to have less stress, more patience, and a more positive outlook on life leading to fewer challenging days.

Every mom's journey in motherhood is unique and these seven mindsets may not apply to everyone in the same way. What's most important is loving your children and doing your best to guide them through life.

Having said that, I want to wrap up with a quick review of each of the seven mindsets we've looked at and how each one impacts your children.

The Seven Mindsets:

1. <u>Growth</u>: Life's dynamic nature means that change is its only constant. The path of motherhood is ever-evolving, often changing, and always offering new perspectives. Being able to embrace a growth mindset is the promise to yourself that no matter what life throws at you, you will rise to the occasion, learn what you need to learn, and change what needs to be changed. Every challenge you face is an opportunity, pushing you to your potential, teaching you resilience, and expanding your horizons. With a growth mindset, as challenges come your way, you see them not as setbacks but as opportunities to grow stronger, wiser, and more resilient. When you model a growth mindset, you become an

emblem of adaptability and perseverance, not just for yourself, but for your children who watch and learn from you. Teaching your children to have a growth mindset is one of the greatest gifts you can give them. Their growth mindset will guide them through life, always knowing they can handle any obstacle or challenge that comes their way.

2. Positivity: In a world teeming with uncertainties, holding onto positivity can seem like clutching at straws during a storm. Motherhood is punctuated with moments of sheer joy and instances of overwhelming doubt. Yet it is positivity that turns the tide, every single time. It's positivity that often acts as the beacon of light in a mom's journey. The power to see a brighter tomorrow, to envision happiness even when it seems elusive, is the mindset of an unstoppable mom. Unstoppable moms have the ability to find the silver lining and to see the rainbow amidst the rain. This ability to focus on the positive is what separates an unstoppable mom from the rest. Harness this mindset by focusing on your blessings, no matter how small, and watch as the world shifts around you, echoing your positive energy. By embracing a positive mindset, you're teaching your child that every storm passes, and every winter is followed by the blossoming of spring. In your optimism lies the blueprint of a hopeful future for your child.

3. Patience and Understanding: The heart of a mom is a sanctuary of patience. Through every sleepless night, every testing tantrum, and every perplexing phase of a growing child, patience and understanding are your anchors. Being a mom often feels like a dance, where you're continually adjusting to the tunes of your child's emotions, needs, and aspirations. It's easy to get overwhelmed, but patience and understanding will guide you through. Every disagreement, every tear, and even every resistance has a reason. Taking a moment to understand, to listen, and to respond with patience can make all the difference. By practicing patience and understanding, you create a nurturing environment where your child

feels valued, heard, and loved. Patience isn't just about waiting; it's how you act while you wait. Your understanding today is building the foundation of a lifelong bond with your child now and forever.

4. <u>Unconditional Love</u>: If there's one thing that defines motherhood, it's boundless, unconditional love. This love is your compass, guiding you through the complexities of raising a child. It's the security blanket that your child wraps themselves in during moments of doubt. Loving unconditionally doesn't just mean loving your child, but also loving the journey of motherhood with all of its ups and downs. Embrace every moment, knowing that your love can heal wounds, bridge gaps, and light up the darkest corners. By loving without conditions, you're planting seeds of self-worth, confidence, and compassion in your child, ensuring they grow into emotionally rich and happy adults

5. <u>Mindful Presence</u>: In an age of distractions, being truly present is perhaps the most significant gift you can give your child. Amidst this chaos, the act of being mindfully present is a gift of unparalleled value. It's not about being there physically, but emotionally, mentally, and spiritually. It's not about the quantity of time but the quality. By immersing yourself in the moment, by listening intently, and by genuinely being there, you create memories that last a lifetime. Cherish every giggle, every story, and every shared moment. Switch off the world outside, even if for a little while, and dive into the world of your child where magic awaits at every turn. By immersing yourself in the 'now', you're engraving memories in the sands of time. Your presence is a testament to your child that they are cherished, valued, and worthy of your undivided attention.

6. <u>Role Modeling</u>: Actions speak louder than words. As mothers, we are the first role model our children look up to. By modeling the values, principles, and lessons we wish to impart, we offer our children a live blueprint to shape their futures. Children are keen observers. They don't just listen; they watch, they mimic, and they learn. When you embody

the values you want to instill in your children, you become their most influential role model. Your actions, choices, and even your resilience in the face of challenges craft the narrative of their learning. Let your actions reflect your teachings. Let your children see in you the strength, resilience, and grace that you wish for them. Being conscious of this influence ensures you pave a path of confidence, caring, and resilience for your children to walk on and follow.

7. <u>Self-Care</u>: Last but by no means least, self-care is the thread that binds all other mindsets together. It's easy to lose yourself amidst the myriad roles played by a mom. An unstoppable mom knows that to pour love, patience, and positivity into her family, she first needs to fill herself up. Taking time for yourself isn't an act of selfishness but one of utmost importance. A rejuvenated, content, and happy mom emanates positivity, patience, love, and warmth. Whether it's a few minutes of quiet meditation, a short walk, or even a hobby you're passionate about, remember to refuel and rejuvenate. After all, a radiant, happy, and healthy mom is the cornerstone of a radiant, happy, and healthy family. By prioritizing self-care, you're also teaching your child the importance of self-love and self-worth.

***

The journey of motherhood is a beautiful tapestry woven with love, resilience, and unyielding strength. These seven mindsets are not distinct but interwoven. They feed into each other, creating a holistic approach to the beautiful, challenging, rewarding journey of motherhood. By embracing them, you're not only fortifying yourself but setting the stage for a legacy of strength, love, and resilience. You're channeling your intrinsic strength and making conscious choices that will echo in the lives of your children and their children.

You are well-equipped with the power of the seven mindsets. Know that you are ready for whatever lies ahead. Embrace each day with open arms, an open heart, and the unwavering belief that you are an unstoppable mom.

Here's to celebrating you, the heartbeats you've shared, the tears you've wiped away, and the infinite moments of joy you've created. Go forth, with the wind beneath your wings, and let the world witness the marvel that is you, an unstoppable mom.

Step forward with confidence, with love, and with an unwavering belief in yourself as you continue on this incredible journey. The world - and your children - need your strength, your grace, and your unique brand of magic.

You've got this!

Chapter Summary

- **The Symphony of Unstoppable Motherhood:** Reflect on your journey through the seven transformative mindsets of motherhood which encapsulate the strength and spirit of being an unstoppable mom.

- **Growth:** Embrace change and challenges as opportunities for growth. Teach resilience and adaptability by modeling a growth mindset.

- **Positivity:** Maintain a positive outlook, focusing on the silver linings and teaching your children the power of optimism.

- **Patience and Understanding:** Demonstrate patience and empathy, understanding your child's perspective and guiding them through life's challenges.

- **Unconditional Love:** Love your children unconditionally, nurturing their self-worth and emotional development.

- **Mindful Presence:** Be fully present with your children, creating lasting memories and deepening your connection.

- **Role Modeling:** Lead by example, modeling the values and behaviors you wish to instill in your children.

- **Self-Care:** Prioritize self-care to maintain your well-being, understanding that it's essential for being the best parent you can be.

- **Your Mindsets Are All Connected:** Recognize that these mindsets are interwoven, each contributing to a holistic approach to motherhood.

- **Embrace the Journey:** Carry these mindsets forward with confidence, knowing they equip you for the diverse experiences of motherhood and give you the tools you need to be an unstoppable mom.

- **Celebrate Unstoppable Motherhood:** Acknowledge your journey, the challenges you've overcome, and the joy you've fostered. Move forward with the knowledge that you are an unstoppable mom, fully able to nurture and inspire your children with your unique strengths and qualities.

Chapter 14

Next Steps: From Inspiration to Action

Navigating Life Beyond this Book as an Unstoppable Mom

> *"Everybody got a mom but nobody got a mom like you."*
> - Author Unknown

Excited about what you've learned and ready for more?

Many moms tell me how helpful this book was to them and ask what they can do next. I love hearing from moms as you all give me so many ideas about what you need and how I can best help you get where you want to go. Since every mom comes from a different place and has different needs, I've designed a few different options. You tell me which one meets you where you are today and I will do my best to help you become the unstoppable mom you want to be.

In addition to joining our active and engaging Facebook group called Be an Unstoppable Mom, you can continue with a self-paced course that digs deeper into the topics we've been talking about and helps you to discover more about who you are and who you want to be. If you want a live, more personal approach to mastering your mindsets and discovering your true self, you can join our online small group coaching program where you will work with me and up to seven other moms as we explore and go into even more depth about your unstoppable mom journey. You'll find camaraderie and support from the group as we spend three months, meeting weekly, learning, and sharing. And if you think one-on-one coaching is where you are at, I offer that too through weekly one-on-one online sessions where we look specifically at you and what you need to become the unstoppable mom you want to be.

Whatever it is you are looking for, I would love to talk with you, learn more about you, and share some of my favorite unstoppable mom tips with you. To schedule a free 30-minute online call with me, visit our Resource page at http://BeAnUnstoppableMom.com/resources and look for the Calendly link where you can schedule a day and time that works for you.

I am here to help you in any way I can. Please reach out and let me know how I can support you.

Join Us on Facebook Today!

Look for the "Be an Unstoppable Mom" group on Facebook.

Ask questions, share your thoughts and ideas, and interact with a group of unstoppable moms, just like you!

I look forward to meeting you there.

And Don't Forget to Visit the Be an Unstoppable Mom Website

This is where I set up an easy to use Resource page for you. You'll find it at: http://www.BeAnUnstoppableMom.com/resources.

You'll also find links to all of the resources mentioned in this book, including links to downloadable PDF files for the Growth Work. Also, when I find new information I think will be helpful to you as an unstoppable mom, I post it in the Bonus section of the Resource page.

Stop by and take a look!

And if you'd like to share your thoughts about this book with other unstoppable moms, please leave a review on Amazon. I appreciate your hearing your feedback.

Made in the USA
Coppell, TX
30 January 2025